Byron

Beauties Gallery

Illustrated

ISBN-13: 978-1495448690

ISBN-10: 149544869X

Dtp
and
graphic design
Iacob Adrian

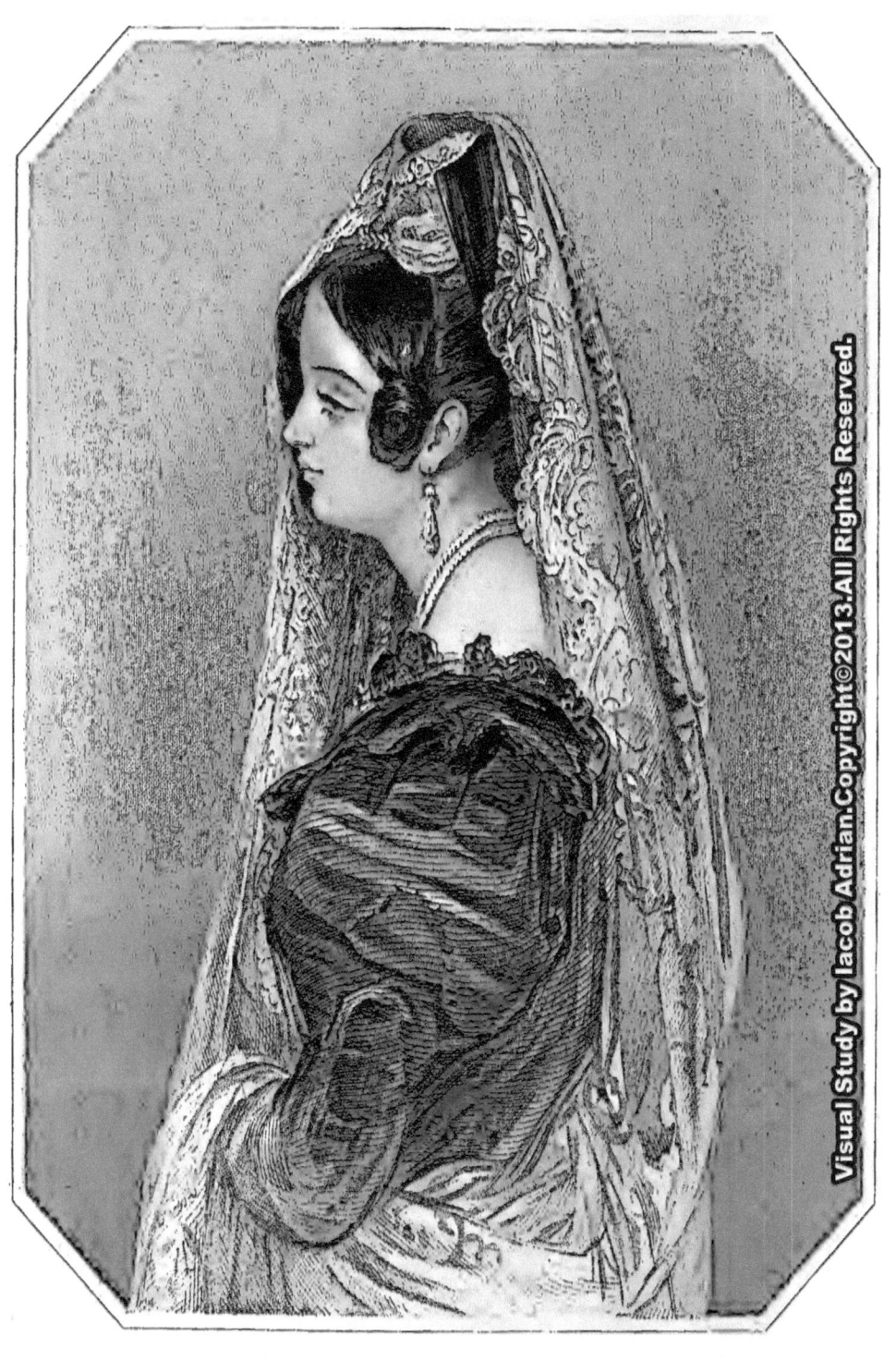

DONNA JULIA.

DONNA JULIA.

——◆——

AMONGST her numerous acquaintance, all
  Selected for discretion and devotion,
There was the Donna Julia, whom to call
  Pretty were but to give a feeble notion
Of many charms in her as natural
  As sweetness to the flower, or salt to ocean,
Her zone to Venus, or his bow to Cupid,
(But this last simile is trite and stupid).

*   *   *   *   *   · *

Her eye (I'm very fond of handsome eyes)
  Was large and dark, suppressing half its fire
Until she spoke, then through its soft disguise
  Flash'd an expression more of pride than ire,
And love than either; and there would arise
  A something in them which was not desire,
But would have been, perhaps, but for the soul
Which struggled through and chasten'd down the whole.

Her glossy hair was cluster'd o'er a brow
  Bright with intelligence, and fair, and smooth;
Her eyebrow's shape was like th' aërial bow,
  Her cheek all purple with the beam of youth,

Mounting, at times, to a transparent glow,
    As if her veins ran lightning; she, in sooth,
Possess'd an air and grace by no means common:
Her stature tall—I hate a dumpy woman.

TENDER and impassioned, but possessing neither information to occupy her intellect, nor good principles to regulate her conduct, Donna Julia is an illustration of the women of Seville, of whom Lord Byron remarked, that "their minds have but one idea, and the business of their lives is intrigue." The slave of every impulse, whether for good or ill, she is represented, as now prostrated before the altar of the Virgin, making the noblest efforts "for honour, pride, religion, virtue's sake;" and then, "in full security of innocence," seeking temptation till "she stood on guilt's steep brink," and found retreat impracticable.

Of her crime, palliated as it is by the influence of national custom, climate, and circumstance, it is difficult to speak with deserved censure, when we witness the suffering consequent upon it, so touchingly described in the letter addressed to her lover, "which breathes," says Mr. Jeffrey, "the very spirit of warm, devoted, pure, unalterable love;" and condemnation is lost in pity, when we follow her in idea to the monastic seclusion in which, an unwilling votaress, her remaining years were spent,

"Where memory lingered o'er the grave of passion,
Watching its tranced sleep."—MATURIN.

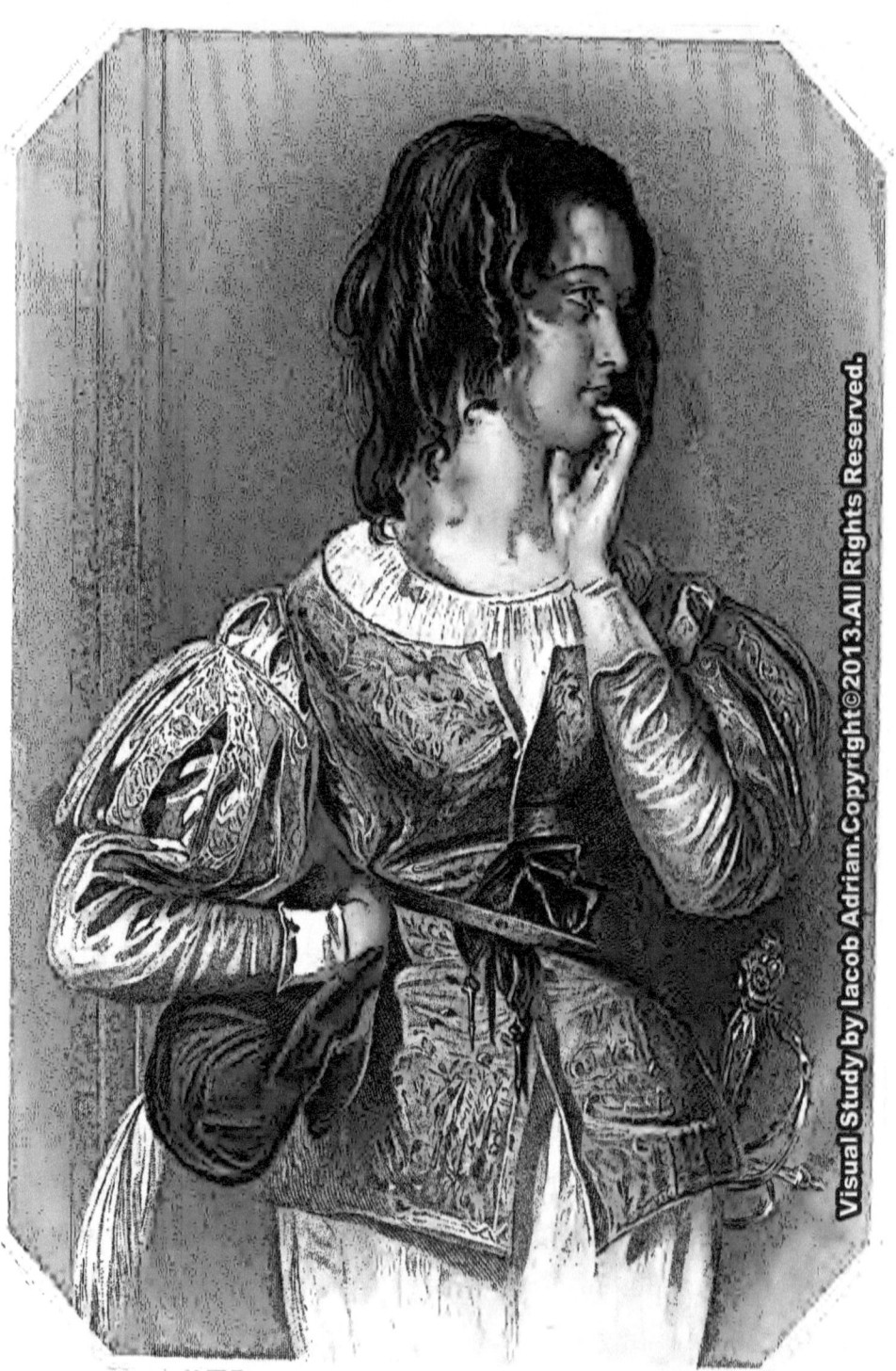

ARMED.

KALED.

Kaled, the "dark page" of Lara, is too familiar with the generality of readers to need any comment. He is depicted by the artist watching his lord in that festival,

"Where long carousal shook th' illumined hall,"

in the palace of Otho. The description of his person is very beautiful.

> Light was his form, and darkly delicate
> That brow whereon his native sun had sate,
> But had not marr'd, though in his beams he grew,
> The cheek where oft the unbidden blush shone through;
> Yet not such blush as mounts when health would show
> All the heart's hue in that delighted glow;
> But 'twas a hectic tint of secret care
> That for a burning moment fever'd there;
> And the wild sparkle of his eye seem'd caught
> From high, and lighten'd with electric thought,
> Though its black orb those long low lashes' fringe
> Had temper'd with a melancholy tinge;
> Yet less of sorrow than of pride was there,
> Or, if 'twere grief, a grief that none should share:
> And pleased not him the sports that please his age,
> The tricks of youth, the frolics of the page;

For hours on Lara he would fix his glance,
As all-forgotten in that watchful trance;
And from his chief withdrawn, he wander'd lone,
Brief were his answers, and his questions none;
His walk the wood, his sport some foreign book;
His resting-place the bank that curbs the brook:
He seem'd, like him he served, to live apart
From all that lures the eye, and fills the heart;
To know no brotherhood, and take from earth
No gift beyond that bitter boon—our birth.

* * * * * *

Of higher birth he seem'd, and better days,
Nor mark of vulgar toil that hand betrays.
So femininely white it might bespeak
Another sex, when match'd with that smooth cheek,
But for his garb, and something in his gaze,
More wild and high than woman's eye betrays;
A latent fierceness that far more became
His fiery climate than his tender frame:
True, in his words it broke not from his breast,
But from his aspect might be more than guess'd.
Kaled his name, though rumour said he bore
Another ere he left his mountain-shore;
For sometimes he would hear, however nigh,
That name repeated loud without reply,
As unfamiliar, or, if roused again,
Start to the sound, as but remember d then;
Unless 'twas Lara's wonted voice that spake,
For then, ear, eyes, and heart would all awake.

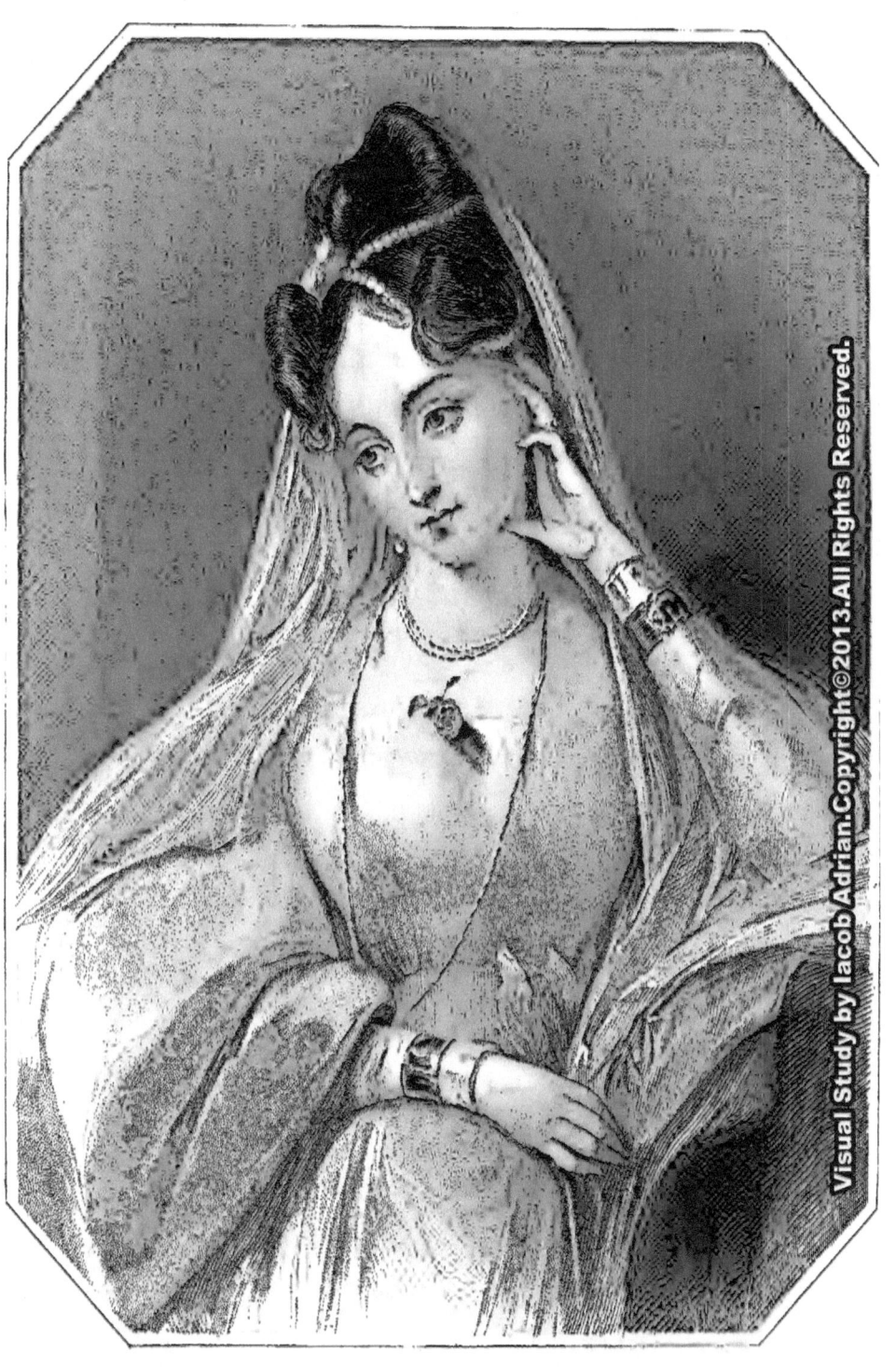

L A U R A .

LAURA.

THE clever and amusing story of Beppo affords a very curious and complete specimen of a kind of diction and composition of which our English has hitherto presented very few examples. It is, in itself, absolutely a thing of nothing—without characters, sentiments, or intelligible object;—a mere piece of lively and loquacious prattling, in short, upon all kinds of frivolous subjects,—a sort of gay and desultory babbling about Italy and England, Turks, balls, literature, and fish sauces. But still there is something very engaging in the uniform gaiety, politeness, and good humour of the author, and something still more striking and admirable in the matchless facility with which he has cast into regular, and even difficult, versification the unmingled, unconstrained, and unselected language of the most light, familiar, and ordinary conversation.

The heroine of the story is thus introduced.

——————'TWAS some years ago,
It may be thirty, forty, more or less,
The carnival was at its height, and so
    Were all kinds of buffoonery and dress;
A certain lady went to see the show,
    Her real name I know not, nor can guess,
And so we'll call her Laura, if you please,
Because it slips into my verse with ease.

LAURA.

She was not old, nor young, nor at the years
  Which certain people call a " *certain age*,"
Which yet the most uncertain age appears,
  Because I never heard, nor could engage
A person yet by prayers, or bribes, or tears,
  To name, define by speech, or write on page,
The period meant precisely by that word,—
Which surely is exceedingly absurd.

Laura was blooming still, had made the best
  Of time, and time return'd the compliment,
And treated her genteelly, so that, dress'd,
  She look'd extremely well where'er she went;
A pretty woman is a welcome guest,
  And Laura's brow a frown had rarely bent:
Indeed she shone all smiles, and seem'd to flatter
Mankind with her black eyes for looking at her.

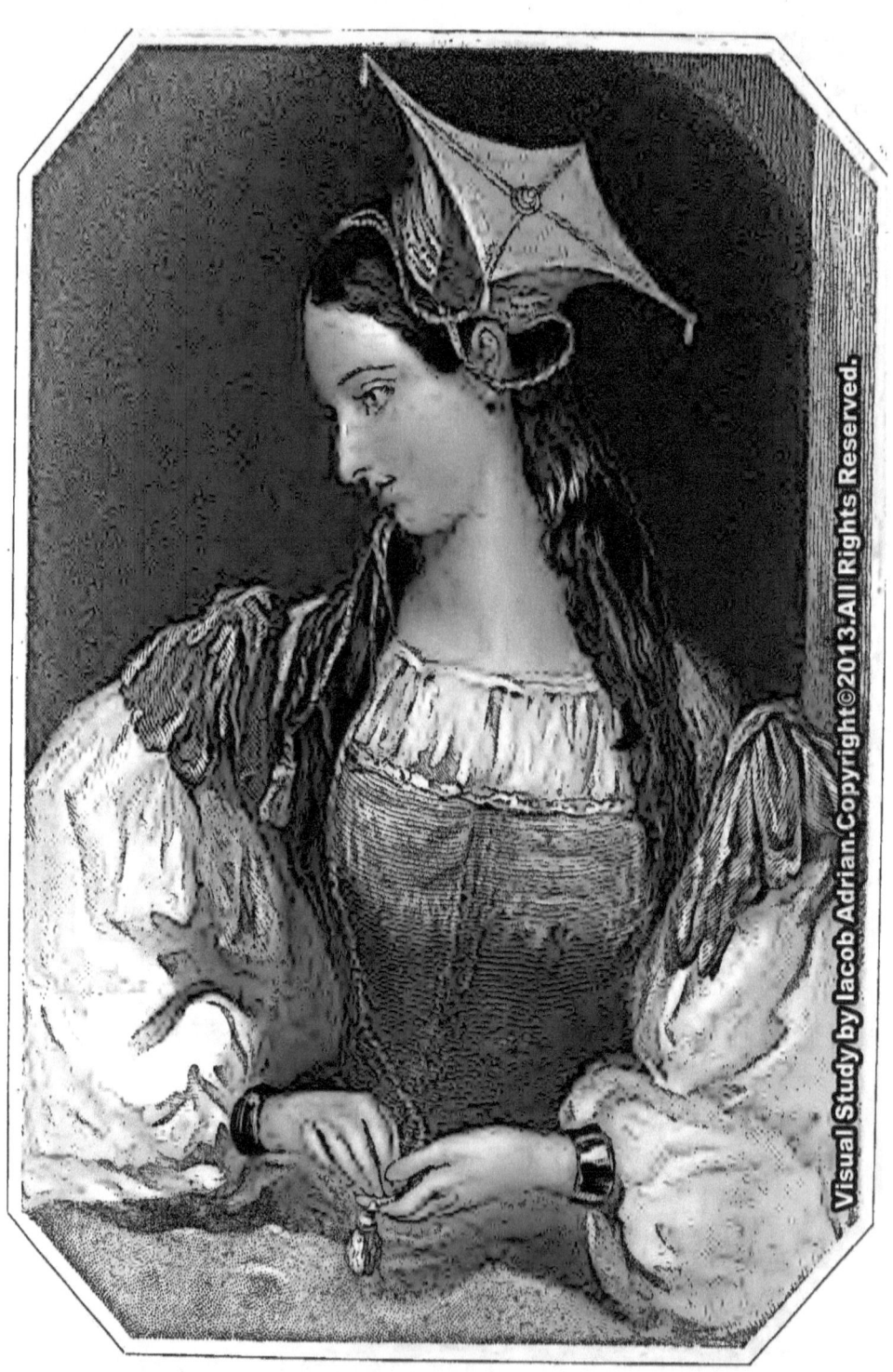

FLORENCE.

FLORENCE.

———◆———

MRS. SPENCER SMITH, who is celebrated in several of Lord
Byron's lesser poems, and apostrophised in Childe Harold, under
the name of "Florence," was the daughter of Baron Herbert,
the Austrian ambassador, and was born at Constantinople during
her father's residence in that city. "Her life," says Lord Byron,
in a letter to his mother from Malta, "has been from its com-
mencement so fertile in remarkable incidents, that in a romance
they would appear improbable. I have found her very pretty,
very accomplished, and extremely eccentric. Since my arrival
here I have had scarcely any other companion." He adds, that
though not yet twenty-five, and unhappily married, she never
had been impeached in point of character.

> SWEET Florence! could another ever share
> This wayward, loveless heart, it would be thine:
> But check'd by every tie, I may not dare
> To cast a worthless offering at thy shrine,
> Nor ask so dear a breast to feel one pang for mine.

> Thus Harold deem'd, as on that lady's eye
> He look'd, and met its beam without a thought,
> Save Admiration glancing harmless by:
> Love kept aloof, albeit not far remote,
> Who knew his votary often lost and caught,

But knew him as his worshipper no more,
And ne'er again the boy his bosom sought:
Since now he vainly urged him to adore,
Well deem'd the little God his ancient sway was o'er.

Fair Florence found, in sooth with some amaze,
One who, 'twas said, still sigh'd to all he saw,
Withstand, unmoved, the lustre of her gaze,
Which others hail'd with real or mimic awe,
Their hope, their doom, their punishment, their law:
All that gay Beauty from her bondsmen claims;
And much she marvell'd that a youth so raw
Nor felt, nor feign'd at least, the oft-told flames,
Which, though sometimes they frown, yet rarely anger dames.

Mr. Moore surmises, with great probability, that Lord Byron's devotion to the lady was that of the imagination, rather than the heart, as in the lines addressed to her in Childe Harold he declares his freedom from even her enthralment; and it is not till absence and distance have added their magic to her fascinations, that his expressions are heightened into tenderness.

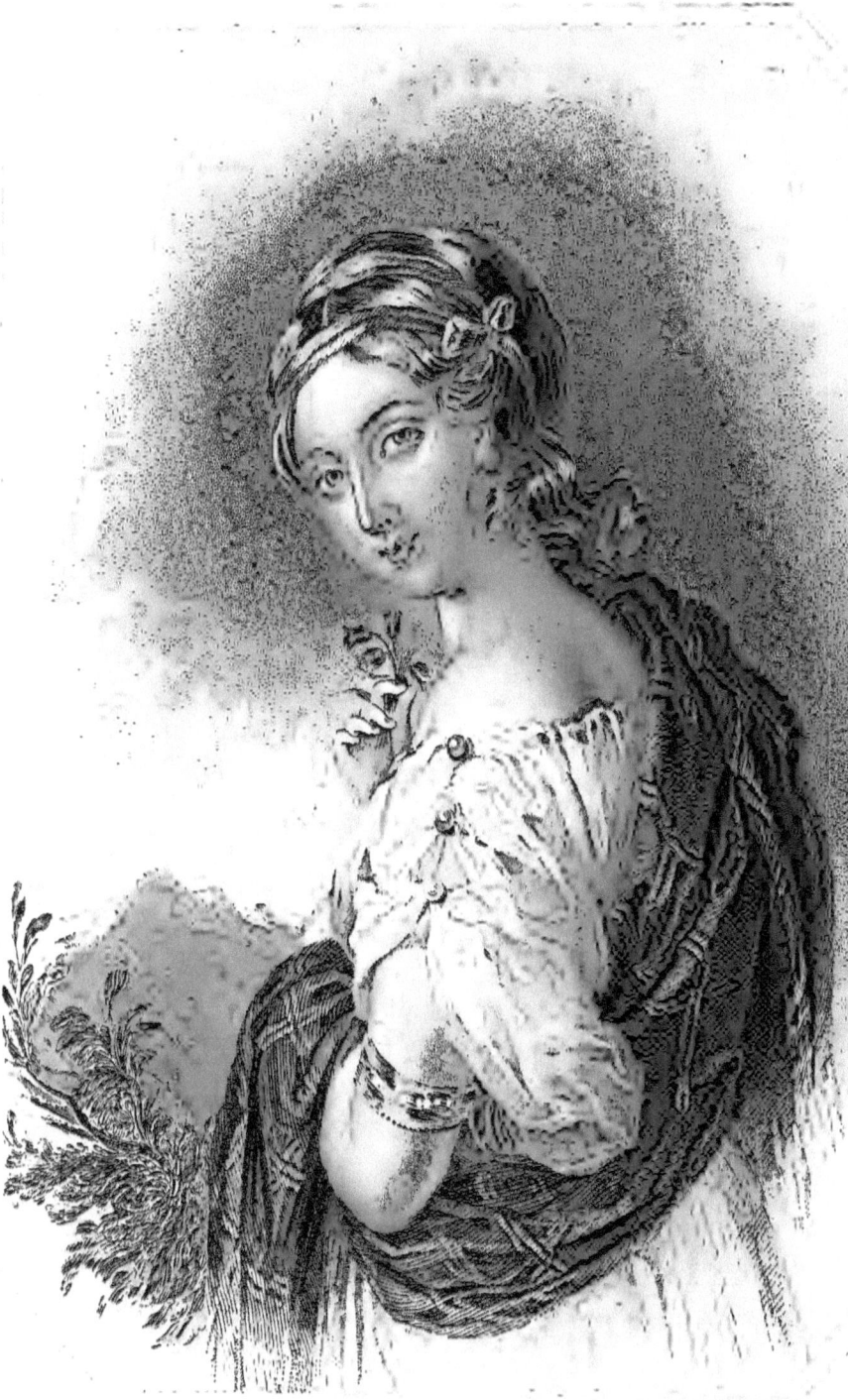

MORA.

MORA.

MORA is the heroine of one of Lord Byron's juvenile productions, named " Oscar of Alva."

FAIR shone the sun on Oscar's birth,
　　When Angus hail'd his eldest born;
The vassals round their chieftain's hearth
　　Crowd to applaud the happy morn.

*　　*　　*　　*　　*　　*

Another year is quickly past,
　　And Angus hails another son;
His natal day is like the last,
　　Nor soon the jocund feast was done.

*　　*　　*　　*　　*　　*

From high Southannon's distant tower
　　Arrived a young and noble dame;
With Kenneth's lands to form her dower,
　　Glenalvon's blue-eyed daughter came;

And Oscar claim'd the beauteous bride,
　　And Angus on his Oscar smiled:
It soothed the father's feudal pride
　　Thus to obtain Glenalvon's child.

Hark to the pibroch's pleasing note !
  Hark to the swelling nuptial song !
In joyous strains the voices float,
  And still the choral peal prolong.

See how the heroes' blood-red plumes
  Assembled wave in Alva's hall ;
Each youth his varied plaid assumes,
  Attending on their chieftain's call.

It is not war their aid demands,
  The pibroch plays the song of peace ;
To Oscar's nuptials throng the bands,
  Nor yet the sounds of pleasure cease.

But where is Oscar ?——

Oscar disappears mysteriously, and is mourned for as dead ;
whilst the fair-haired Allan, his younger brother, stimulated by
the hope of possessing the broad lands of the disconsolate lady,
undertakes the office of consoler, and succeeds so well, that,
after some period has elapsed, the festivities are begun which are
meant to celebrate his marriage with Mora. A dark unbidden
guest, however, demands a pledge to the lost Oscar, alive or
dead. All drink the health but Allan, the guilty brother, who
is denounced by the stranger as the murderer of Oscar.

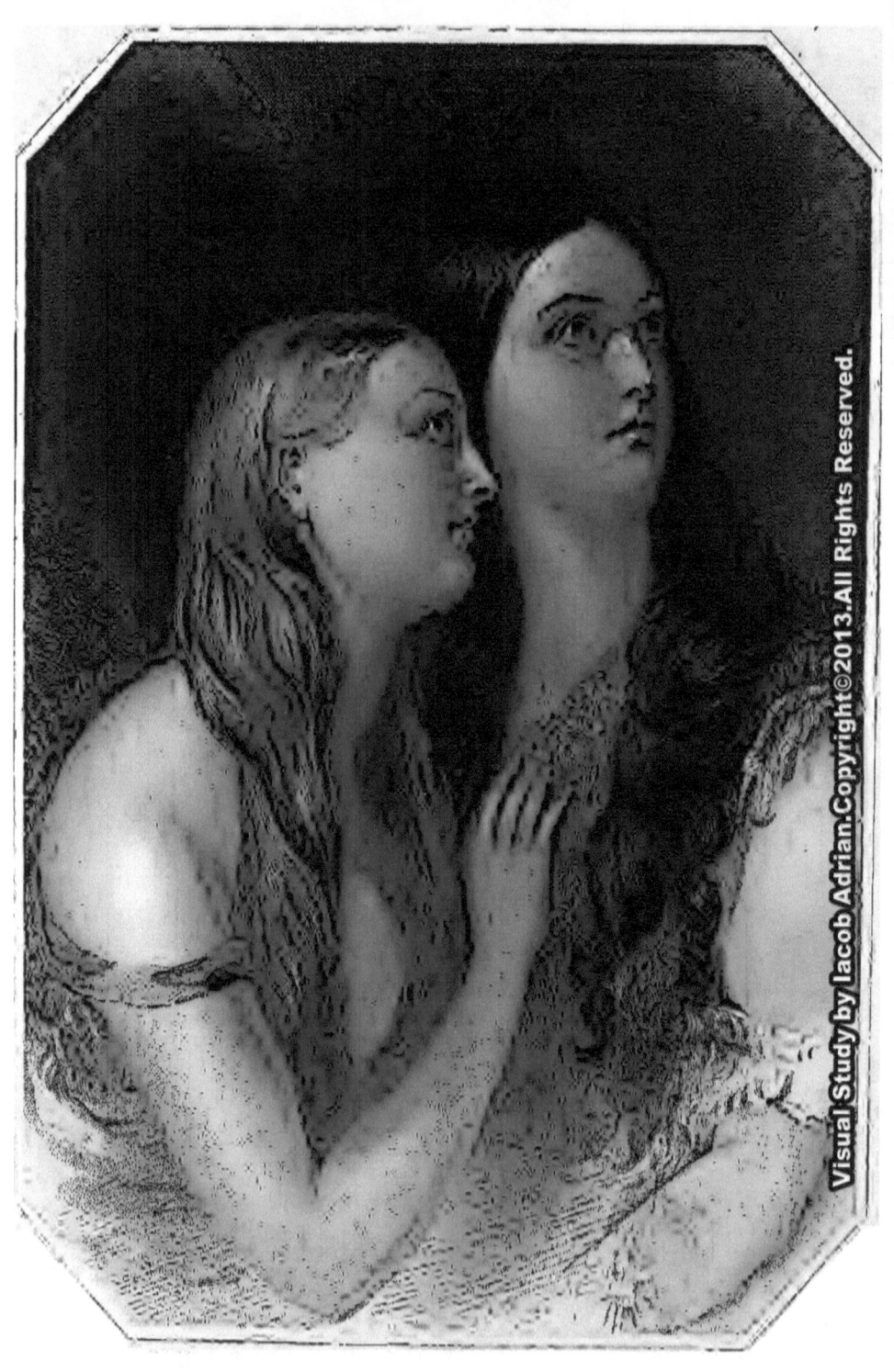

ANAH AND AHOLIBAMAH.

ANAH AND AHOLIBAMAH.

" THE first scene of this splendid Mystery (Heaven and
Earth,) is a woody and mountainous district, near Mount
Ararat ; the time midnight. Mortal creatures, conscious of their
own wickedness, have heard awful predictions of the threatened
flood, and all their lives are darkened with terror. But the sons
of God have been dwellers on earth, and women's hearts have
been stirred by the beauty of these celestial visitants. Anah and
Aholibamah, two of these angel-stricken maidens, come wandering
along while others sleep, to pour forth their invocations to their
demon lovers. They are of very different characters: Anah,
soft, gentle, and submissive ; Aholibamah, proud, impetuous,
and aspiring—the one loving in fear, and the other in ambition."

In the engraving, the sisters, their invocation ended, are
represented as watching the descent of their lovers.

> *Anah.* SISTER ! sister ! I view them winging
> Their bright way through the parted night.
> *Aholibamah.* The clouds from off their pinions flinging,
> As though they bore to-morrow's light.
> *Anah.* But if our father see the sight!
> *Aho.* He would but deem it was the moon
> Rising unto some sorcerer's tune
> An hour too soon.

ANAH AND AHOLIBAMAH.

Anah. They come! *he* comes!—Azaziel!

Aho.   Haste

To meet them! Oh! for wings to bear
My spirit, while they hover there,
To Samiasa's breast!

    Anah. Lo! they have kindled all the west,
Like a returning sunset;—lo
  On Ararat's late secret crest
A mild and many-colour'd bow,
The remnant of their flashing path,
Now shines! and now, behold! it hath
Return'd to night, as rippling foam,
  Which the leviathan hath lash'd
From his unfathomable home,
When sporting on the face of the calm deep,
  Subsides soon after he again hath dash'd
Down, down, to where the ocean's fountains sleep.

    Aho. They have touch'd earth! Samiasa!

    Anah.   My Azaziel!

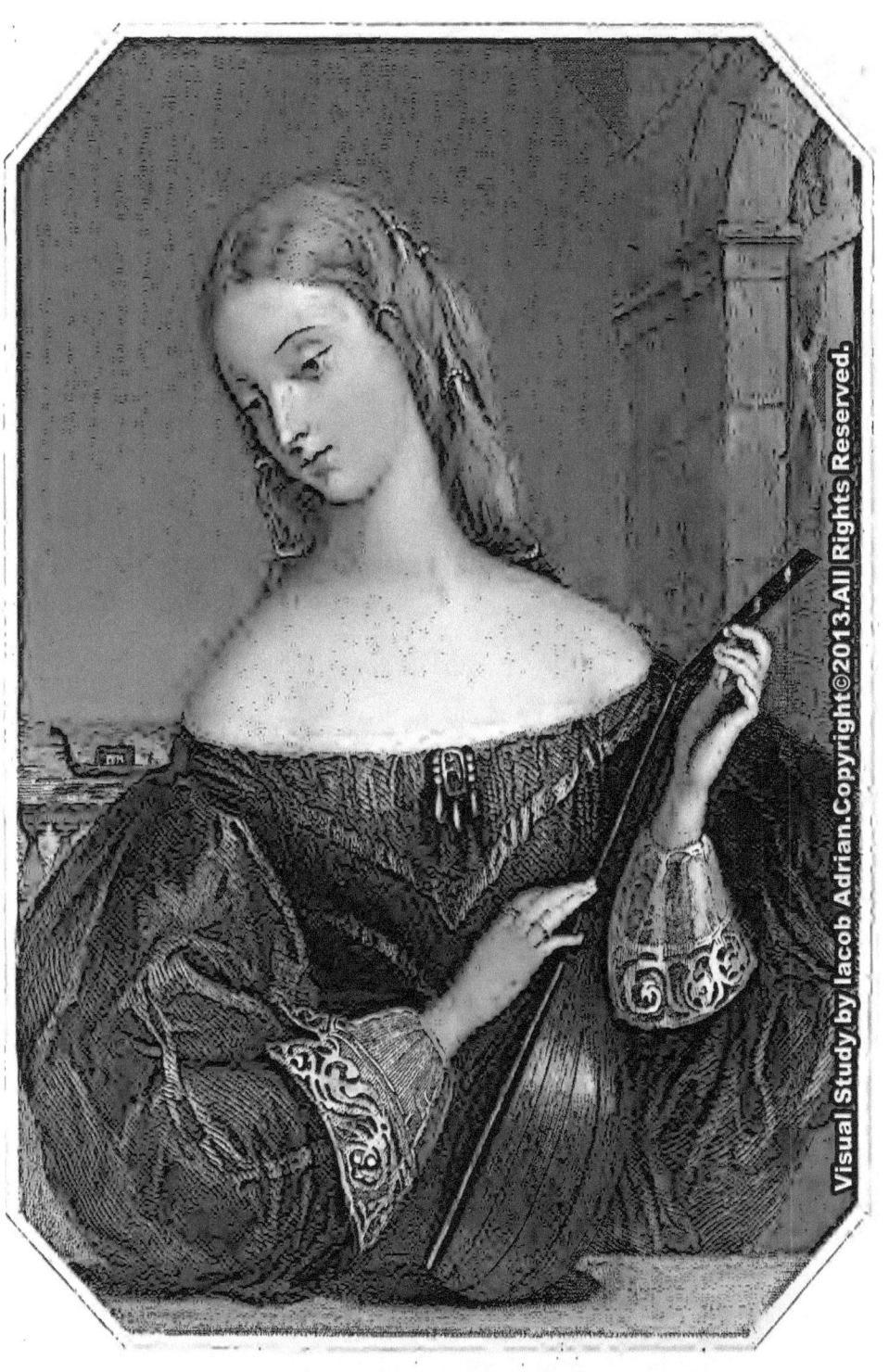

ANGIOLINA.

ANGIOLINA.

THE whole of the scene from which the following lines are taken, is so beautiful, that we wish we could extract more largely. The little we have room for will illustrate, perhaps better than any other passage we could select, the pure mind of Angiolina, a being too innocent herself to credit the existence of guilt in others.

Marino.   And do you love him?

Angiolina. I love all noble qualities which merit
Love, and I loved my father, who first taught me
To single out what we should love in others,
And to subdue all tendency to lend
The best and purest feelings of our nature
To baser passions. He bestow'd my hand
Upon Faliero: he had known him noble,
Brave, generous; rich in all the qualities
Of soldier, citizen, and friend; in all
Such have I found him as my father said.
His faults are those that dwell in the high bosoms
Of men who have commanded; too much pride,
And the deep passions fiercely foster'd by
The uses of patricians, and a life
Spent in the storms of state and war; and also
From the quick sense of honour, which becomes

A duty to a certain sign, a vice
When overstrain'd, and this I fear in him
And then he has been rash from his youth upwards,
Yet temper'd by redeeming nobleness
In such sort, that the wariest of republics
Has lavish'd all its chief employs upon him,
From his first fight to his last embassy,
From which on his return the dukedom met him.

Mar. But previous to this marriage, had your heart
Ne'er beat for any of the noble youth,
Such as in years had been more meet to match
Beauty like yours ? or since have you ne'er seen
One, who, if your fair hand were still to give,
Might now pretend to Loredano's daughter?

Ang. I answer'd your first question when I said
I married.

Mar.   And the second?

Ang.   Needs no answer.

Mar. I pray you pardon, if I have offended.

Ang. I feel no wrath, but some surprise: I knew not
That wedded bosoms could permit themselves
To ponder upon what they *now* might choose,
Or aught save their past choice.

Mar.   'Tis their past choice
That far too often makes them deem they would
Now choose more wisely, could they cancel it.

Ang. It may be so.   I knew not of such thoughts.

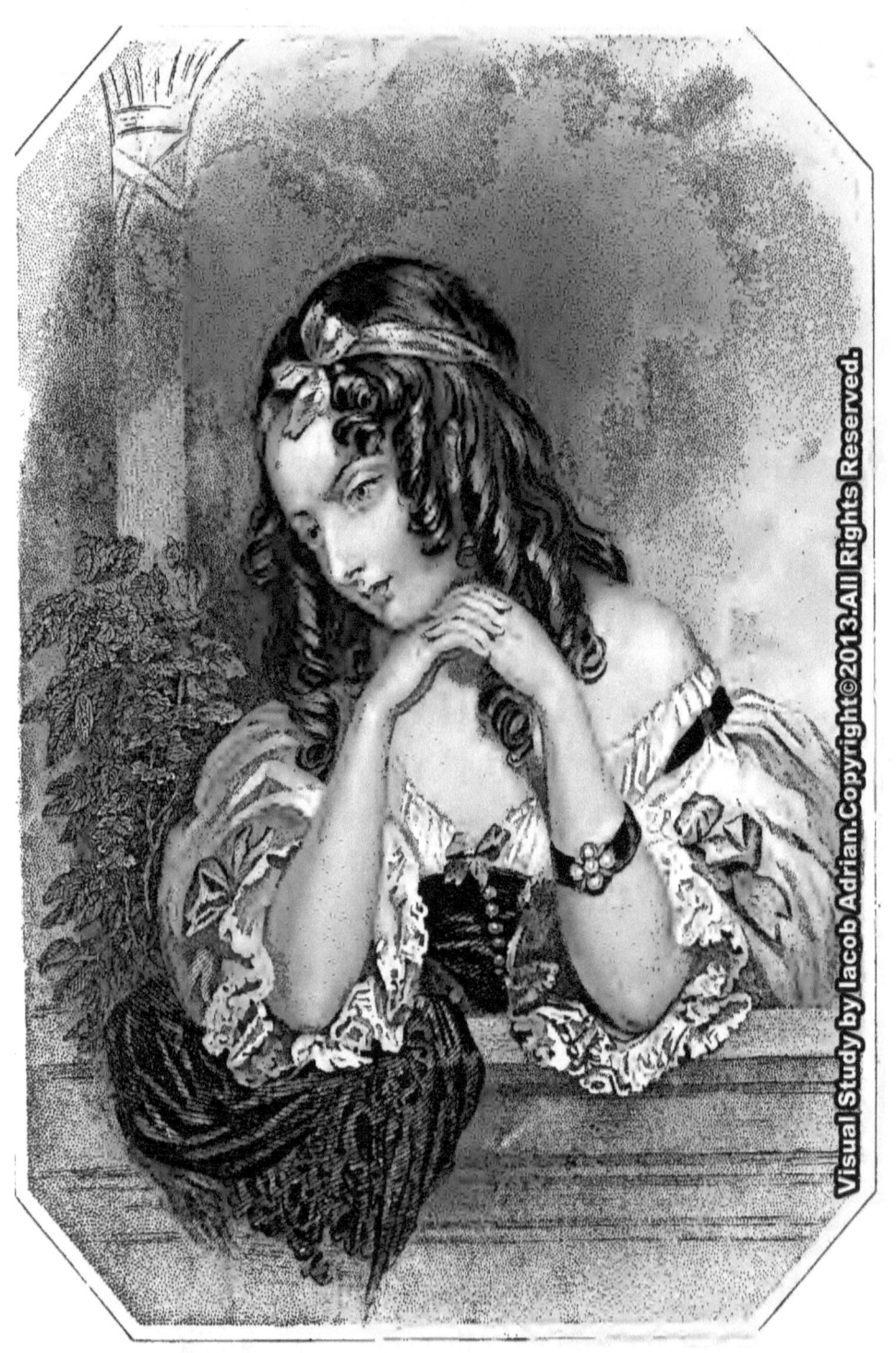

MARION.

MARION.

—◆—

DOUBTLESS another of the poet's juvenile heroines—one too cold—and perhaps too satirically disposed, to please his warm and youthful imagination.

MARION! why that pensive brow?
What disgust to life hast thou?
Change that discontented air;
Frowns become not one so fair.
'Tis not love disturbs thy rest,
Love's a stranger to thy breast;
He in dimpling smiles appears,
Or mourns in sweetly timid tears,
Or bends the languid eyelid down,
But shuns the cold forbidding frown.
Then resume thy former fire,
Some will love, and all admire;
While that icy aspect chills us,
Nought but cool indifference thrills us.
Wouldst thou wandering hearts beguile,
Smile at least, or seem to smile.
Eyes like thine were never meant
To hide their orbs in dark restraint;

Spite of all thou fain wouldst say,
Still in truant beams they play.

* * * * * *

Marion, adieu! oh, prithee slight not
This warning, though it may delight not;
And lest my precepts be displeasing
To those who think remonstrance teasing,
At once I'll tell thee our opinion
Concerning woman's soft dominion:
Howe'er we gaze with admiration
On eyes of blue or lips carnation,
Howe'er the flowing locks attract us,
Howe'er those beauties may distract us,
Still fickle, we are prone to rove,
These cannot fix our souls to love:
It is not too severe a stricture
To say they form a pretty picture:
But wouldst thou see the secret chain
Which binds us in your humble train,
To hail you queens of all creation,
Know, in a word, 'tis ANIMATION.

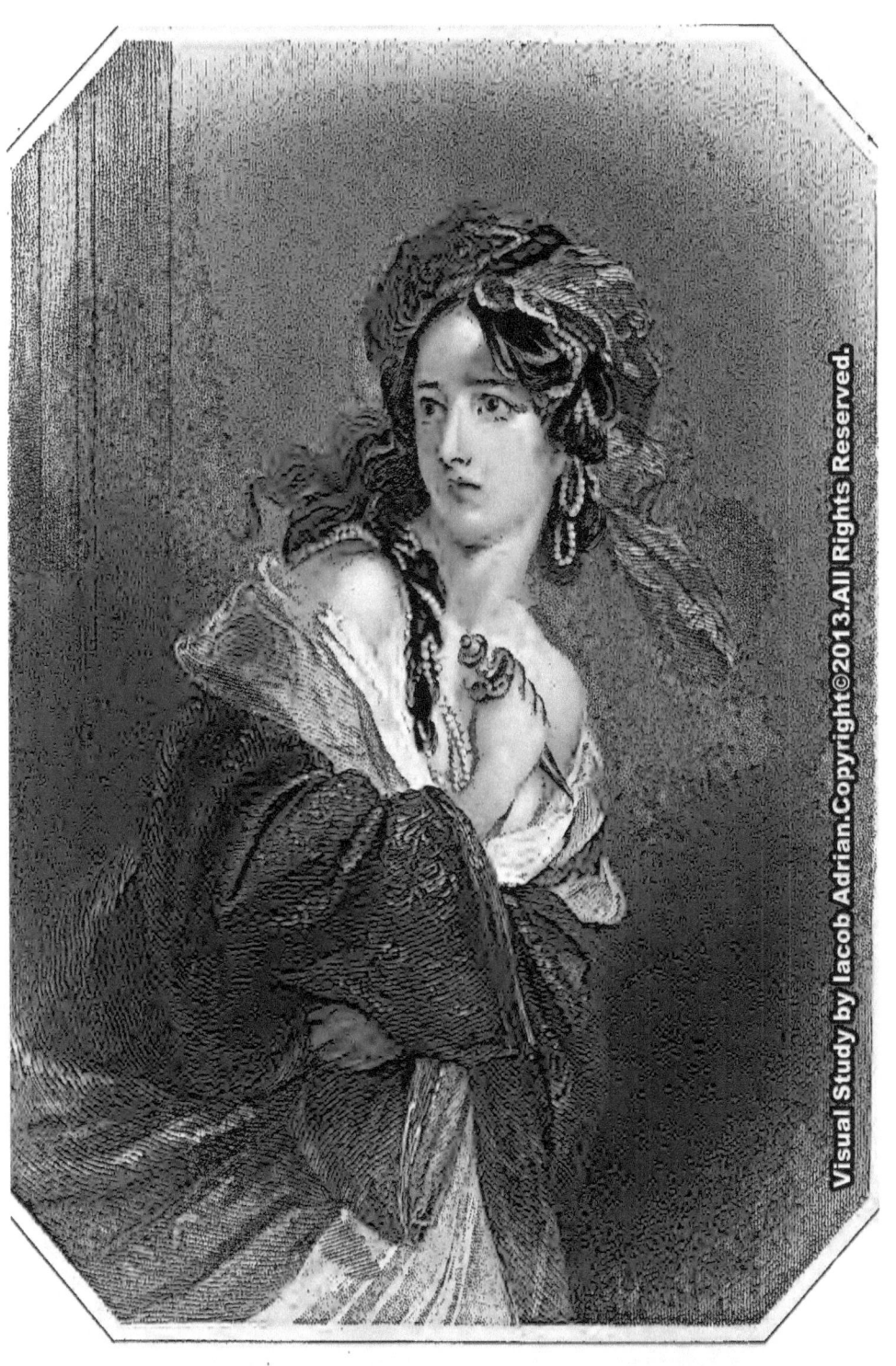

GULNARE.

GULNARE.

HAVING failed in his enterprise, Conrad is thrown into the dungeon of the Pacha, Seyd. He is waked from his slumbers by Gulnare, who confesses her love for him, and her determination to effect his escape. Four days pass on. At midnight "that fair she" returns, and urges Conrad to assassinate his enemy and fly; but he refuses to lift his arm against a defenceless foe. Again she persuades, but without avail; till at length in desperation she resolves herself to strike the blow, which will at once free her from her hated master, and open the prison-door of her slighting lover.

> SHE turn'd, and vanish'd ere he could reply,
> But his glance followed far with eager eye:
> And gathering, as he could, the links that bound
> His form, to curl their length, and curb their sound,
> Since bar and bolt no more his steps preclude,
> He, fast as fetter'd limbs allow, pursued.
> 'Twas dark and winding, and he knew not where
> That passage led; nor lamp nor guard were there:
> He sees a dusky glimmering—shall he seek
> Or shun that ray so indistinct and weak?
> Chance guides his steps—a freshness seems to bear
> Full on his brow, as if from morning air—

He reach'd an open gallery—on his eye
Gleam'd the last star of night, the clearing sky:
Yet scarcely heeded these—another light
From a lone chamber struck upon his sight.
Towards it he moved; a scarcely closing door
Reveal'd the ray within, but nothing more.
With hasty step a figure outward past,
Then paused—and turned—and paused—'tis She at last!
No poniard in that hand—nor sign of ill—
" Thanks to that softening heart—she could not kill ! "
Again he look'd, the wildness of her eye
Starts from the day abrupt and fearfully.
She stopp'd—threw back her dark far-floating hair,
That nearly veil'd her face and bosom fair:
As if she late had bent her leaning head
Above some object of her doubt or dread.
They meet—upon her brow—unknown—forgot—
Her hurrying hand had left—'twas but a spot—
Its hue was all he saw, and scarce withstood—
Oh ! slight but certain pledge of crime—'tis blood !

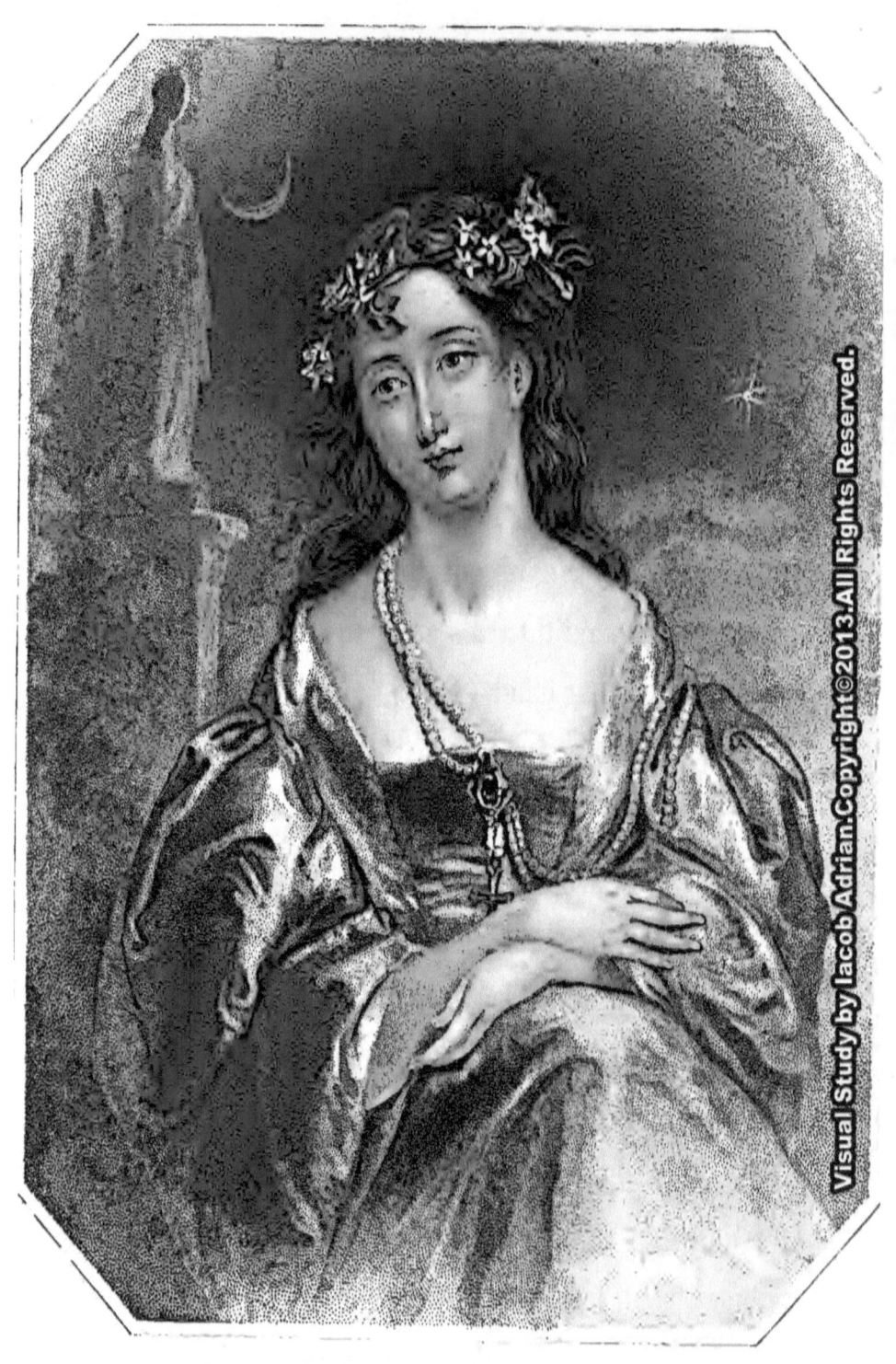

GENEVRA.

GENEVRA.

—◆—

FROM the following extract from Lord Byron's diary it would seem, that he was unconscious of the exquisite beauty of his sonnets to Genevra. "Redde some Italian, and wrote two sonnets. I never wrote but one sonnet before, and that was not in earnest, and many years ago, as an exercise—and I will never write another. They are the most puling, petrifying, stupidly platonic compositions."

SONNET I.

THINE eyes' blue tenderness, thy long fair hair,
   And the wan lustre of thy features —caught
   From contemplation—where serenely wrought,
Seems Sorrow's softness charm'd from its despair—
Have thrown such speaking sadness in thine air,
   That—but I know thy blessed bosom fraught
   With mines of unalloy'd and stainless thought—
I should have deem'd thee doom'd to earthly care.
With such an aspect, by his colours blent,
   When from his beauty-breathing pencil born,
(Except that *thou* hast nothing to repent)
   The Magdalen of Guido saw the morn—
Such seem'st thou—but how much more excellent!
With nought Remorse can claim—nor Virtue scorn.

GENEVRA.

SONNET II.

Thy cheek is pale with thought, but not from woe,
   And yet so lovely, that if Mirth could flush
   Its rose of whiteness with the brightest blush,
My heart would wish away that ruder glow:
And dazzle not thy deep-blue eyes—but, oh!
   While gazing on them sterner eyes will gush,
   And into mine my mother's weakness rush,
Soft as the last drops round heaven's airy bow.
For, through thy long dark lashes low depending,
   The soul of melancholy Gentleness
Gleams like a seraph from the sky descending,
   Above all pain, yet pitying all distress;
At once such majesty with sweetness blending,
   I worship more, but cannot love thee less.

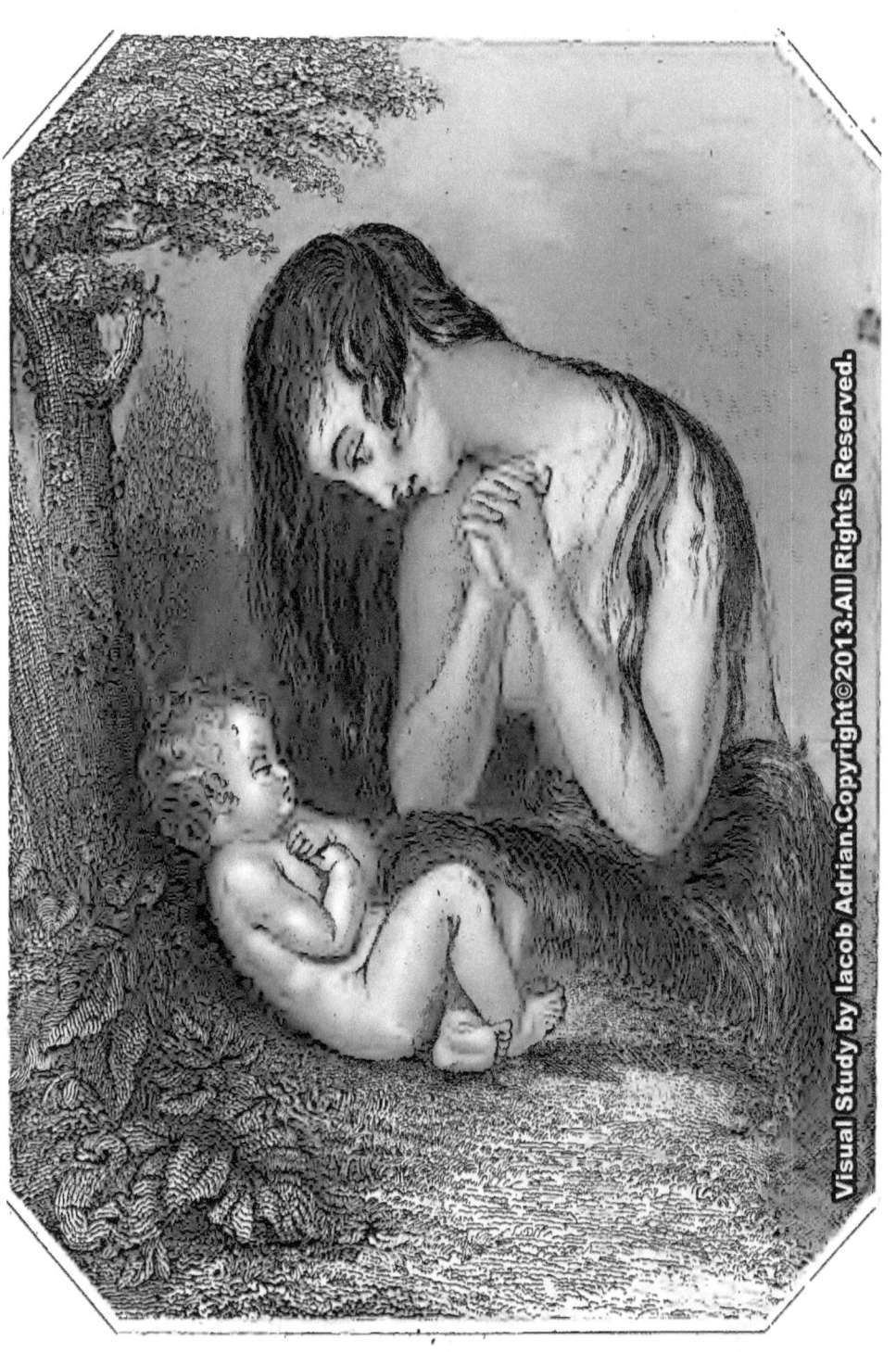

ADAH.

ADAH.

"THE censorious may say what they will," says Sir Egerton Brydges, "but there are speeches in the mouth of Cain and Adah, especially regarding their child, which nothing in English poetry, but the 'wood notes wild' of Shakspeare ever equalled." The picture speaks for itself.

Adah. Hush! tread softly, Cain.

Cain.   I will; but wherefore?

Adah. Our little Enoch sleeps upon yon bed
Of leaves, beneath the cypress.

Cain.   Cypress! 'tis
A gloomy tree, which looks as if it mourn'd
O'er what it shadows; wherefore didst thou choose it
For our child's canopy?

Adah.   Because its branches
Shut out the sun like night, and therefore seem'd
Fitting to shadow slumber.

Cain.   Ay, the last—
And longest; but no matter—lead me to him.

                    [*They go up to the child.*

How lovely he appears! his little cheeks,
In their pure incarnation, vying with
The rose leaves strewn beneath them.

Adah.   And his lips, too,
How beautifully parted! No; you shall not
Kiss him, at least not now : he will awake soon—
His hour of mid-day rest is nearly over ;
But it were pity to disturb him till
'Tis closed.

    Cain.   You have said well; I will contain
My heart till then.   He smiles and sleeps !—Sleep on
And smile, thou little, young inheritor
Of a world scarce less young : sleep on, and smile !
Thine are the hours and days when both are cheering
And innocent! *thou* hast not pluck'd the fruit—
Thou know'st not thou art naked !   Must the time
Come thou shalt be amerced for sins unknown,
Which were not thine nor mine ?   But now sleep on !
His cheeks are reddening into deeper smiles,
And shining lids are trembling o'er his long
Lashes, dark as the cypress which waves o'er them ;
Half open, from beneath them the clear blue
Laughs out although in slumber.   He must dream—
Of what ?   Of Paradise !—Ay ! dream of it,
My disinherited boy !   'Tis but a dream !

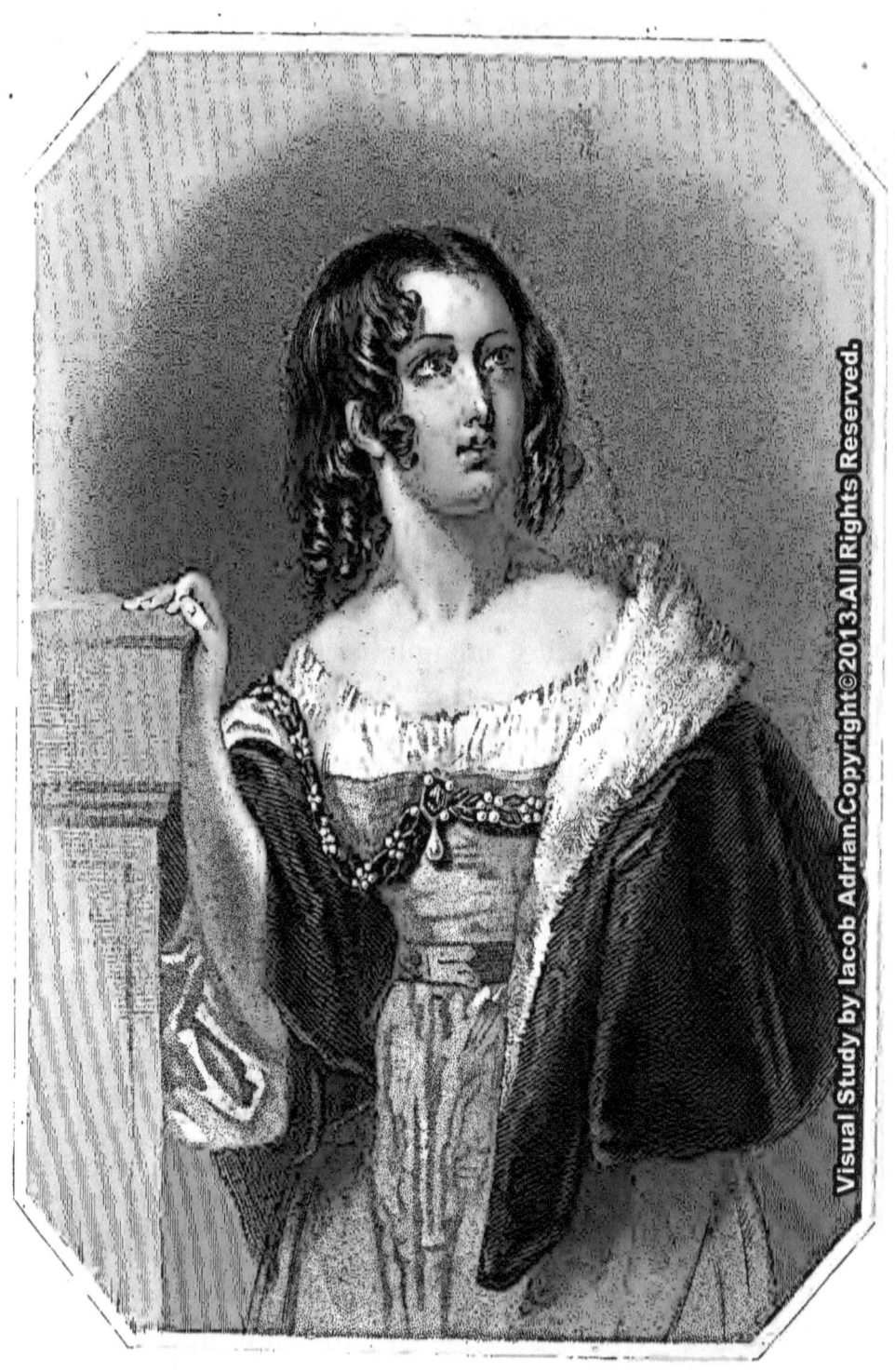

CAROLINE.

CAROLINE.

—◆—

THREE of Lord Byron's juvenile poems are addressed to . Caroline, the first of which, as most expressive of the feelings which animated his young and ardent mind, we subjoin. There is no allusion to Caroline in Mr. Moore's life, and the scenes of youthful fondness so elegantly described by the poet, were probably unknown to others, or unnoticed at the time, and live now only in the remembrance of the object of them, if indeed she have not already followed the footsteps of her lover to those "dark mountains," where—

"None have saluted, and none have replied."

Each of the poems seems to have been written about the year 1805, when Byron was in his sixteenth year.

I.

THINK'ST thou I saw thy beauteous eyes,
  Suffused in tears, implore to stay;
And heard unmoved thy plenteous sighs,
  Which said far more than words can say?

II.

Though keen the grief thy tears exprest,
　　When love and hope lay both o'erthrown ;
Yet still, my girl, this bleeding breast
　　Throbb'd with deep sorrow as thine own.

III.

But when our cheeks with anguish glow'd,
　　When thy sweet lips were joined to mine,
The tears that from my eyelids flow'd
　　Were lost in those which fell from thine.

IV.

Thou couldst not feel my burning cheek,
　　Thy gushing tears had quenched its flame,
And as thy tongue essay'd to speak,
　　In sighs alone it breath'd my name.

V.

And yet, my girl, we weep in vain,
　　In vain our fate in sighs deplore ;
Remembrance only can remain,—
　　But that will make us weep the more.

VI.

Again, thou best beloved, adieu ;
　　Ah ! if thou canst, o'ercome regret,
Nor let thy mind past joys review,—
　　Our only hope is to forget !

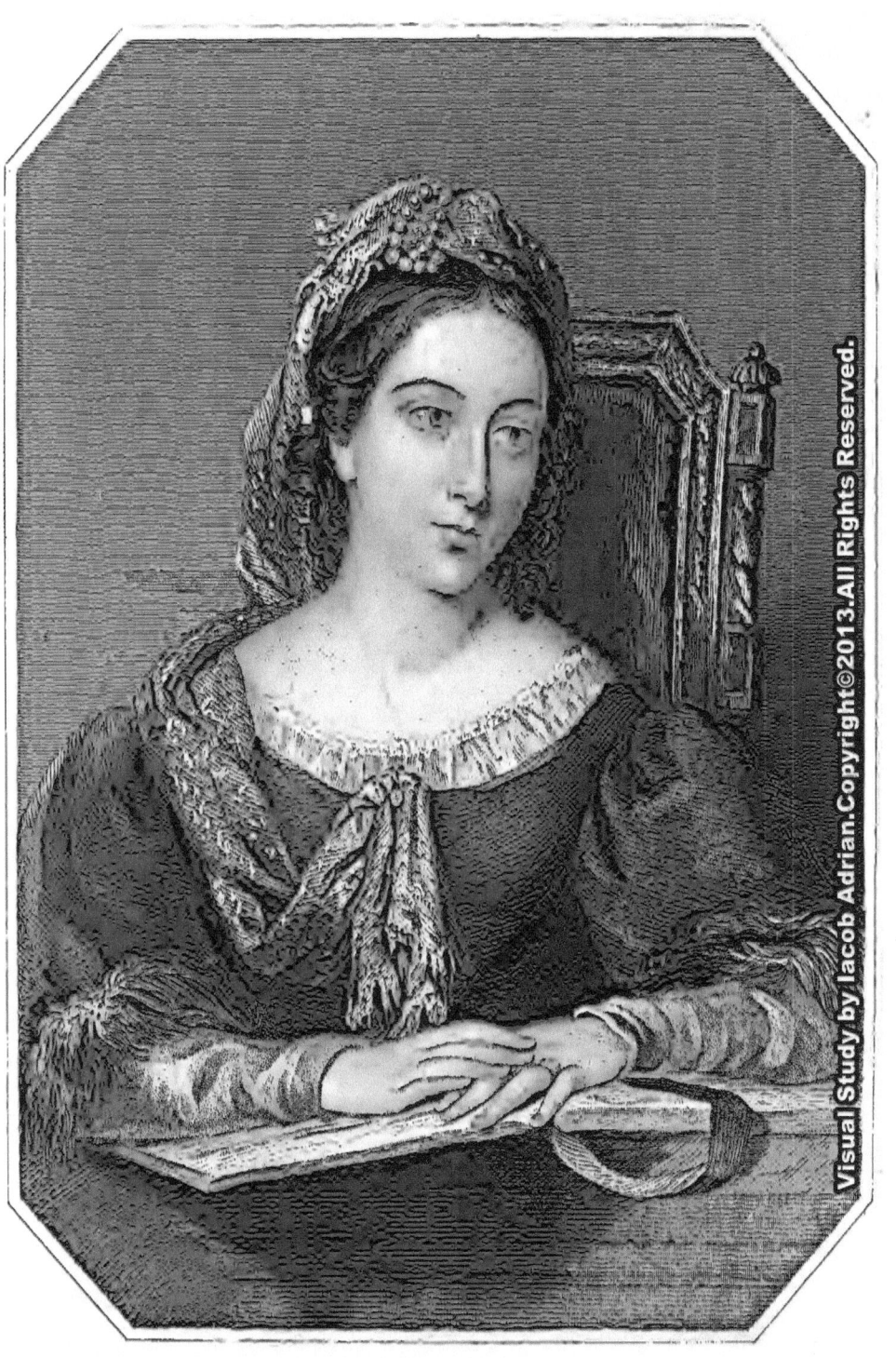

BEATRICE.

BEATRICE.

According to Boccaccio, Dante was a lover long before he was a soldier, and his passion for the Beatrice whom he has immortalised, commenced when he was in his ninth year, and she in her eighth year. It is said that their first meeting was at a banquet in the house of Folco Portinaro, her father; and certain it is, that the impression then made on the susceptible and constant heart of Dante was not obliterated by her death, which happened after an interval of sixteen years. His regret for her loss was probably increased by the domestic unhappiness consequent on his union with Gemma Donati,

> —————————— that fatal she,
> —————————— the cold partner, who hath brought
> Destruction for a dowry.

The following beautiful address to Beatrice is the opening passage of Lord Byron's " Prophecy of Dante :"—

> Once more in man's frail world! which I had left
> So long that 'twas forgotten; and I feel
> The weight of clay again,—too soon bereft
> Of the immortal vision which could heal
> My earthly sorrows, and to God's own skies
> Lift me from that deep gulf without repeal,
> Where late my ears rung with the damned cries
> Of souls in hopeless bale; and from that place
> Of lesser torment, whence men may arise

Pure from the fire to join the angelic race;
    Midst whom my own bright Beatricè bless'd
    My spirit with her light; and to the base
Of the eternal Triad! first, last, best,
    Mysterious, three, sole, infinite, great God!
    Soul universal! let the mortal guest,
Unblasted by the glory, though he trod
    From star to star to reach the almighty throne.
    Oh, Beatricè! whose sweet limbs the sod
So long hath press'd, and the cold marble stone,
    Thou sole pure seraph of my earliest love,
    Love so ineffable, and so alone,
That nought on earth could more my bosom move,
    And meeting thee in heaven was but to meet
    That without which my soul, like the arkless dove,
Had wander'd still in search of, nor her feet
    Relieved her wing till found; without thy light
    My paradise had still been incomplete.
Since my tenth sun gave summer to my sight
    Thou wert my life, the essence of my thought,
    Loved ere I knew the name of love, and bright
Still in these dim old eyes, now overwrought
    With the world's war, and years, and banishment,
    And tears for thee, by other woes untaught;
For mine is not a nature to be bent
    By tyrannous faction, and the brawling crowd,
    And though the long, long conflict hath been spent
In vain, and never more, save when the cloud
    Which overhangs the Apennine, my mind's eye
    Pierces to fancy Florence, once so proud
Of me, can I return, though but to die,
    Unto my native soil, they have not yet
    Quench'd the old exile's spirit, stern and high.

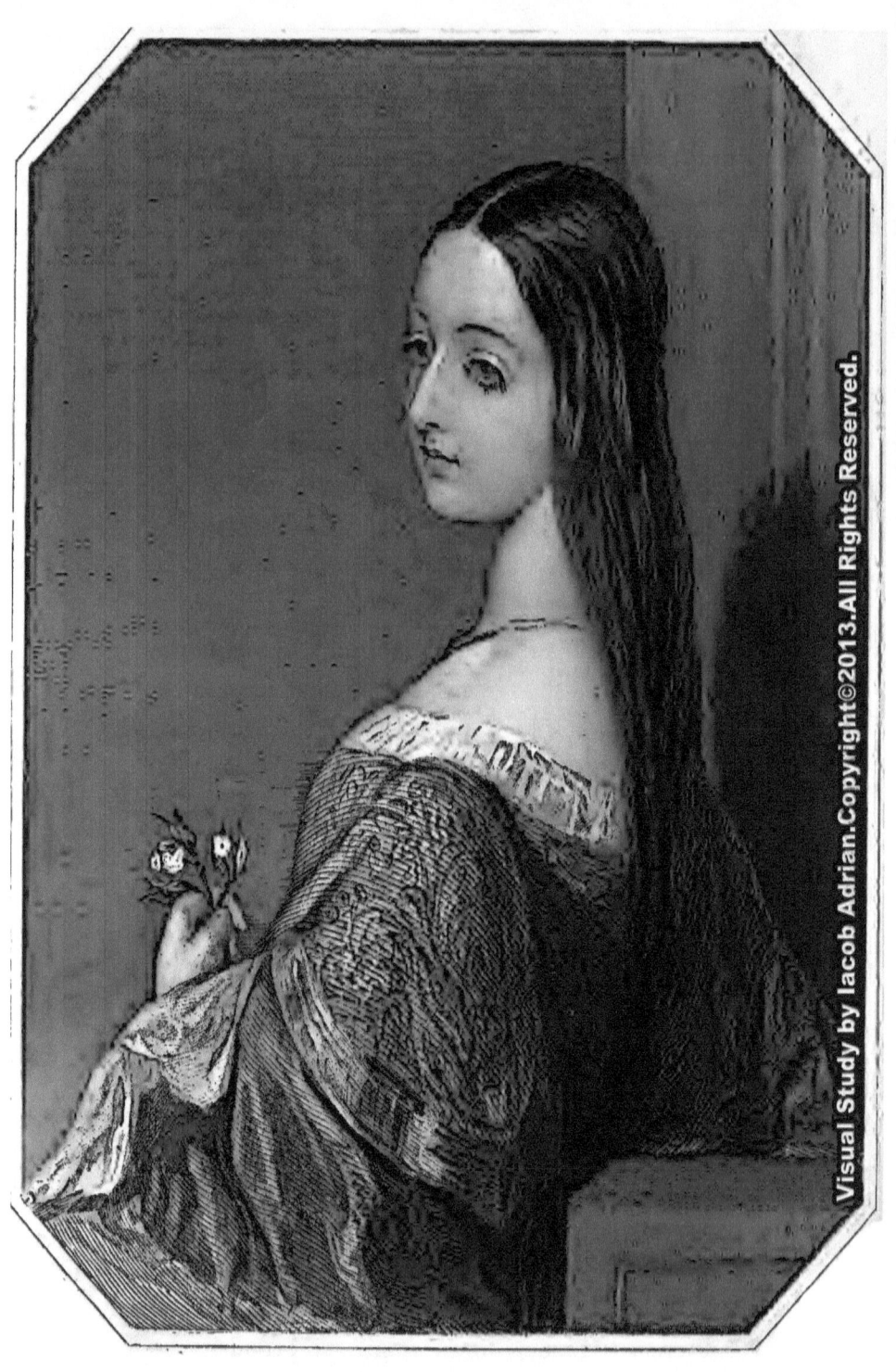

LEONORA D'ESTÉ.

LEONORA D'ESTÈ.

It is the proud privilege of genius to outlive the remembrance of the combined attractions of royalty, power, wealth, learning, and beauty. Leonora d'Estè, the "bright particular star," who was in 1585 too much above her lover to receive from him any but the most distant worship, in 1835 shines solely from the borrowed light of Tasso's genius, and is associated in our recollections only with the poet of Jerusalem.

Leonora, sister of Alphonso II., the Duke of Ferrara, was wise and generous, and not only well read in elegant literature, but even versed in the more abstruse sciences. Having refused the most advantageous offers of marriage, she resided with Lauretta, Duchess of Urbino, her elder sister, who was separated from her husband. Tasso is supposed to allude to his passion for Leonora, in the beautiful episode of Sopronia and Olindo, in the second book of his celebrated poem, where he gives a fine description of her person and character, and a touching account of his own unregarded devotion and hopeless love.

Perhaps Leonora, though too proud and chaste to encourage the passion of Tasso, was not insensible to his merit ; for we learn, that of the many friends to whom he wrote to petition for his return to Ferrara, none answered the banished and disgraced poet but the princess. Her kindness, however, was fatal to its object.   He returned to the court, was arrested by order of Alphonso, conducted to the hospital of Saint Anna, and confined in a solitary cell as a maniac.

THEY call'd me mad—and why?
Oh, Leonora! wilt not *thou* reply?
I was indeed delirious in my heart
To lift my love so lofty as thou art;
But still my frenzy was not of the mind;
I knew my fault, and feel my punishment
Not less because I suffer it unbent.
That thou wert beautiful, and I not blind,
Hath been the sin which shuts me from mankind;
But let them go, or torture as they will,
My heart can multiply thine image still;
Successful love may sate itself away,
The wretched are the faithful; 'tis their fate
To have all feeling save the one decay,
And every passion into one dilate,
As rapid rivers into ocean pour;
But ours is fathomless, and hath no shore.

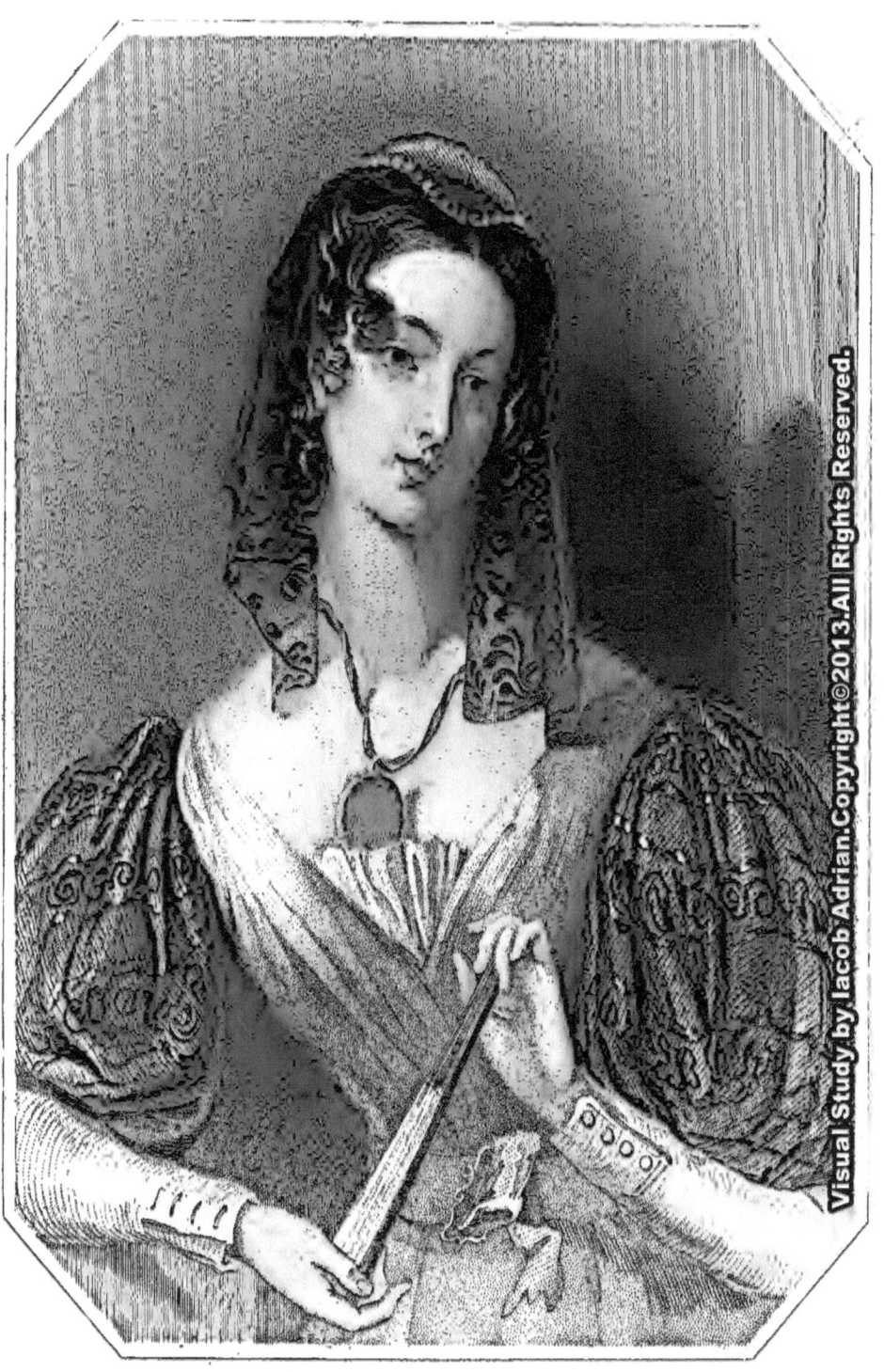

I N E Z.

INEZ.

It was to Inez that Lord Byron addressed those melancholy stanzas in the first canto of Childe Harold, beginning,

"Nay, smile not at my sullen brow!"

which contain, says Mr. Moore, "some of the dreariest touches of sadness that ever Byron's pen let fall." In the first draught of the canto we find a gayer poem, which had probably more reference to the person addressed, and from which we extract the following stanzas, descriptive of the Spanish beauty:—

Oh never talk again to me
    Of northern climes and British ladies;
It has not been your lot to see,
    Like me, the lovely girl of Cadiz.
Although her eye be not of blue,
    Nor fair her locks, like English lasses,
How far its own expressive hue
    The languid azure eye surpasses!

Prometheus-like, from heaven she stole
    The fire, that through those silken lashes
In darkest glances seems to roll,
    From eyes that cannot hide their flashes:

And as along her bosom steal
    In lengthen'd flow her raven tresses,
You'd swear each clustering lock could feel,
    And curl'd to give her neck caresses.

* Our English maids are long to woo,
    And frigid even in possession;
And if their charms be fair to view,
    Their lips are slow at Love's confession:
But born beneath a brighter sun,
    For love ordain'd the Spanish maid is,
And who,—when fondly, fairly won,—
    Enchants you like the Girl of Cadiz?

And when, beneath the evening star,
    She mingles in the gay Bolero,
Or sings to her attuned guitar
    Of Christian knight or Moorish hero;
Or counts her beads with fairy hand
    Beneath the twinkling rays of Hesper,
Or joins devotion's choral band,
    To chaunt the sweet and hallow'd vesper;—

In each her charms the heart must move
    Of all who venture to behold her;
Then let not maids less fair reprove
    Because her bosom is not colder:
Through many a clime 'tis mine to roam
    Where many a soft and melting maid is,
But none abroad, and few at home,
    May match the dark-eyed Girl of Cadiz.

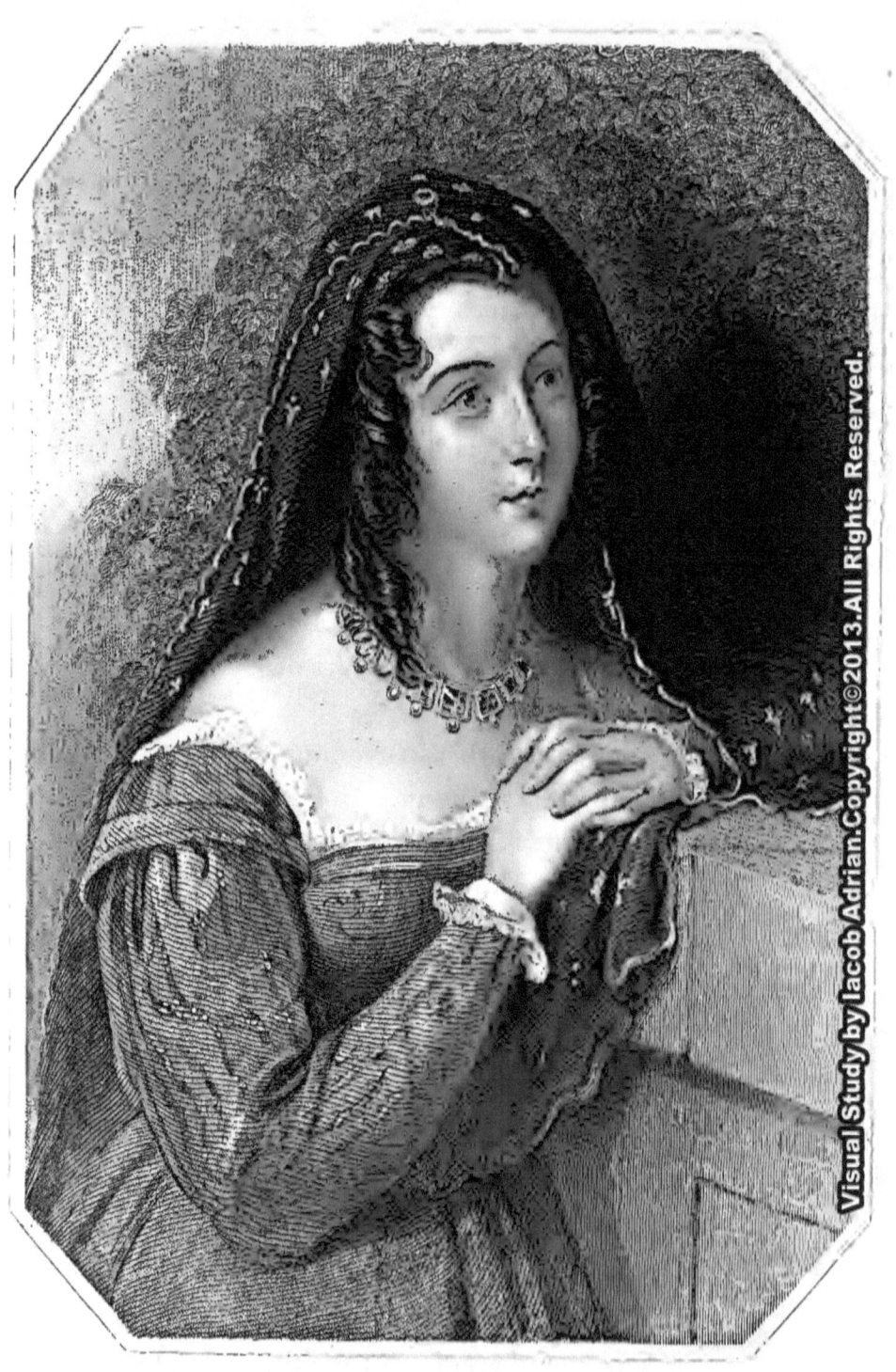

PARISINA.

PARISINA.

THE following poem, says Lord Byron, is grounded on a circumstance mentioned in Gibbon's "Antiquities of the House of Brunswick." I am aware, that in modern times the delicacy or fastidiousness of the reader may deem such subjects unfit for the purposes of poetry. The Greek dramatists, and some of the best of our old English writers, were of a different opinion: as Alfieri and Schiller have also been, more recently, upon the Continent. The following extract will explain the facts on which the story is founded. The name of *Azo* is substituted for Nicholas as more metrical.

"Under the reign of Nicholas III. Ferrara was polluted with a domestic tragedy. By the testimony of an attendant, and his own observation, the Marquis of Este discovered the incestuous loves of his wife Parisina, and Hugo his bastard son, a beautiful and valiant youth. They were beheaded in the castle by the sentence of a father and husband, who published his shame, and survived their execution. He was unfortunate, if they were guilty: if they were innocent, he was still more unfortunate; nor is there any possible situation in which I can sincerely approve the last act of the justice of a parent."

The painter has represented Parisina waiting, in the soft hour of twilight, the approach of her lover.

I.

It is the hour when from the boughs
  The nightingale's high note is heard;
It is the hour when lovers' vows
  Seem sweet in every whisper'd word
And gentle winds, and waters near,
Make music to the lonely ear.
Each flower the dews have lightly wet,
And in the sky the stars are met,
And on the wave is deeper blue,
And on the leaf a browner hue,
And in the heaven that clear obscure,
So softly dark, and darkly pure,
Which follows the decline of day,
As twilight melts beneath the moon away.

II.

But it is not to list to the waterfall
That Parisina leaves her hall,
And it is not to gaze on the heavenly light
That the lady walks in the shadow of night;
And if she sits in Este's bower,
'Tis not for the sake of its full-blown flower—
She listens—but not for the nightingale—
Though her ear expects as soft a tale.
There glides a step through the foliage thick,
And her cheek grows pale—and her heart beats quick.
There whispers a voice through the rustling leaves,
And her blush returns, and her bosom heaves:
A moment more—and they shall meet—
'Tis past—her lover's at her feet.

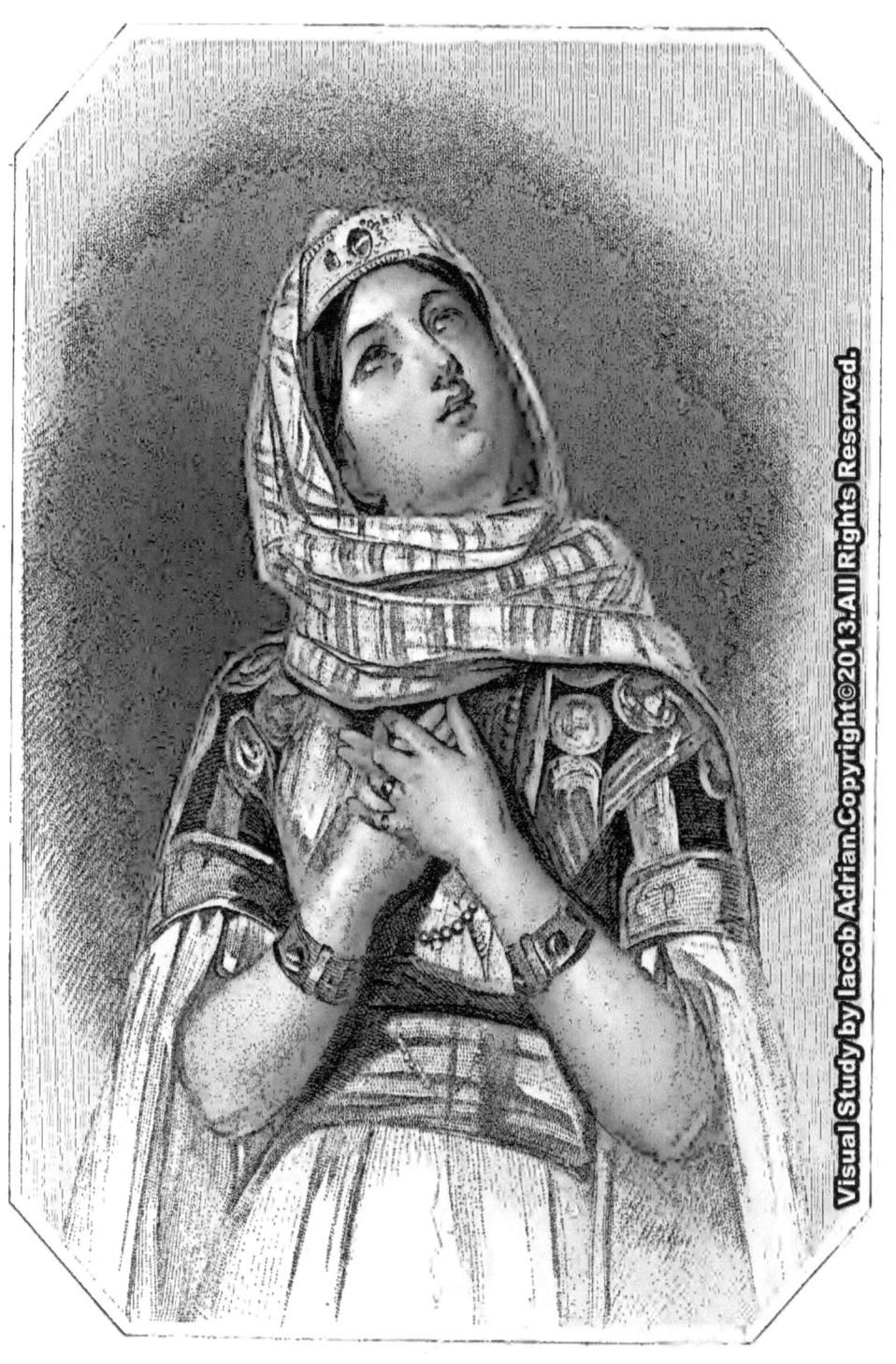

JEPHTHAS DAUGHTER.

JEPHTHA'S DAUGHTER.

"BEFORE Jephtha went forth against the Ammonites, he made the memorable vow, that, if he returned victorious, he would sacrifice as a burnt offering whatever first met him on his entrance into his native city. He gained a splendid victory. At the news of it, his only daughter came dancing forth, in the gladness of her heart, and with jocund instruments of music, to salute the deliverer of his people. The miserable father rent his clothes in agony; but the noble-spirited maiden would not hear of the disregard of the vow: she only demanded a short period to bewail upon the mountains, like the Antigone of Sophocles, her dying without hope of becoming a bride or mother, and then submitted to her fate."

Lord Byron's touching lines are supposed to be addressed by the maiden to her father, at the moment previous to the sacrifice.

I.

SINCE our Country, our God—Oh, my Sire!
Demand that thy Daughter expire;
Since thy triumph was bought by thy vow—
Strike the bosom that 's bared for thee now!

II.

And the voice of my mourning is o'er,
And the mountains behold me no more :
If the hand that I love lay me low,
There cannot be pain in the blow.

III.

And of this, oh, my Father! be sure—
That the blood of thy child is as pure
As the blessing I beg ere it flow,
And the last thought that soothes me below.

IV.

Though the virgins of Salem lament,
Be the judge and the hero unbent!
I have won the great battle for thee,
And my Father and Country are free !

V.

When this blood of thy giving hath gush'd,
When the voice that thou lovest is hush'd,
Let my memory still be thy pride,
And forget not I smiled as I died!

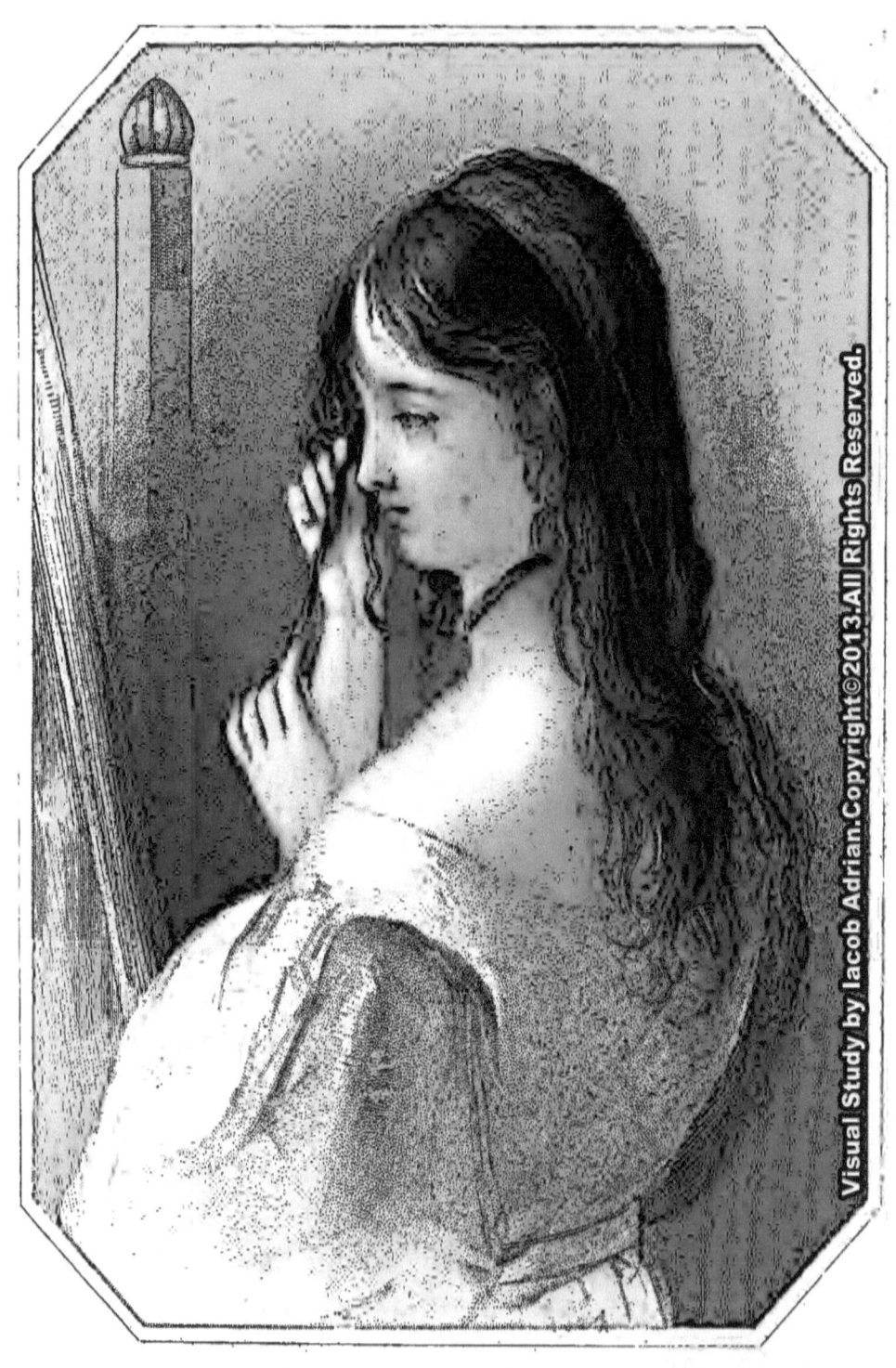

JULIE.

JULIE.

———✦———

RoussEAU's Julie has been enshrined, like the worthless forms in amber, in one of the finest poems in our language, and has thereby derived an interest, of which, among English readers, it had otherwise been destitute. Those persons who, being familiar with Lord Byron's eloquent description of the genius of Rousseau, should turn for confirmation of its truth to the most celebrated novel by that author,—would feel, we think, as the child, who, having looked through the tube of the kaleidoscope, and admired

> " Its hues like sunbeams, dazzling as they past,"

proceeds to investigate its construction, and discovers only broken glass, and worthless beads and pebbles.

> But this is not my theme; and I return
> To that which is immediate, and require
> Those who find contemplation in the urn,
> To look on One, whose dust was once all fire,
> A native of the land where I respire
> The clear air for a while—a passing guest,
> Where he became a being,—whose desire
> Was to be glorious; 'twas a foolish quest,
> The which to gain and keep, he sacrificed all rest.

> Here the self-torturing sophist, wild Rousseau,
> The apostle of Affliction, he who threw
> Enchantment over passion, and from woe
> Wrung overwhelming eloquence, first drew

The breath which made him wretched; yet he knew
How to make madness beautiful, and cast
O'er erring deeds and thoughts a heavenly hue
Of words, like sunbeams, dazzling as they past
The eyes, which o'er them shed tears feelingly and fast.

His love was passion's essence—as a tree
On fire by lightning; with ethereal flame
Kindled he was, and blasted; for to be
Thus, and enamour'd, were in him the same.
But his was not the love of living dame,
Nor of the dead who rise upon our dreams,
But of ideal beauty, which became
In him existence, and o'erflowing teems
Along his burning page, distemper'd though it seems.

This breathed itself to life in Julie, this
Invested her with all that's wild and sweet;
This hallow'd, too, the memorable kiss
Which every morn his fever'd lip would greet,
From hers, who but with friendship his would meet;
But to that gentle touch, through brain and breast
Flash'd the thrill'd spirit's love-devouring heat;
In that absorbing sigh perchance more blest
Than vulgar minds may be with all they seek possest.

The Countess d'Houdetot, the prototype of Julie, was of a pale complexion, and of a graceful figure, with beautiful light brown hair, which was worn, at the period, falling over the shoulders. Her near-sightedness gave her an expression of uncertainty and timidity, which produced a charming mixture of *gaucherie* and grace; and her mind and feelings lighted up her countenance with an ever-varying expression.

Rousseau was accustomed to walk every morning to a considerable distance, that he might receive from Julie the single kiss, which was the ordinary salutation among French acquaintance.

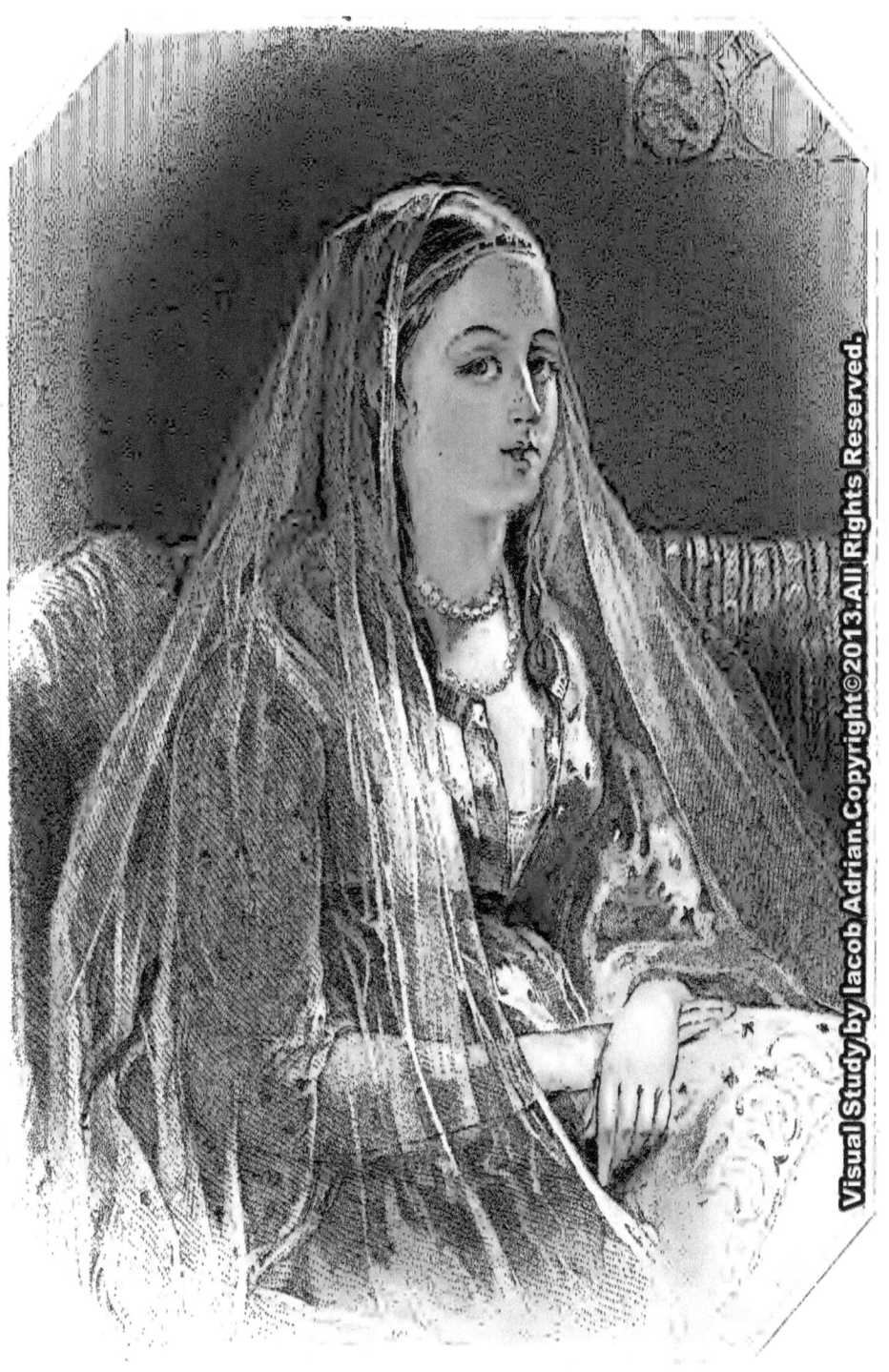

KATINKA.

KATINKA.

INTERRUPTED by the entrance of the sultan, Don Juan, still in feminine disguise, retires to the seraglio, where he is welcomed as a new comer by its fair inhabitants. Of these, the subjects of this and the following engraving, are Katinka and Dudù.

AND yet they had their little jealousies.
   Like all the rest; but upon this occasion,
Whether there are such things as sympathies
   Without our knowledge or our approbation,
Although they could not see through his disguise,
   All felt a soft kind of concatenation,
Like magnetism, or devilism, or what
You please—we will not quarrel about that:

But certain 'tis they all felt for their new
   Companion something newer still, as 't were
A sentimental friendship through and through,
   Extremely pure, which made them all concur
In wishing her their sister, save a few
   Who wish'd they had a brother just like her,
Whom, if they were at home in sweet Circassia,
They would prefer to Padisha or Pacha.

KATINKA.

Of those who had most genius for this sort
  Of sentimental friendship, there were three,
Lolah, Katinka, and Dudù, in short,
  (To save description) fair as fair can be
Were they, according to the best report,
  Though differing in stature and degree,
And clime and time, and country and complexion;
They all alike admired their new connection.

Lolah was dusk as India and as warm;
  Katinka was a Georgian, white and red,
With great blue eyes, a lovely hand and arm,
  And feet so small they scarce seem'd made to tread,
But rather skim the earth; while Dudù's form
  Look'd more adapted to be put to bed,
Being somewhat large, and languishing, and lazy,
Yet of a beauty that would drive you crazy.

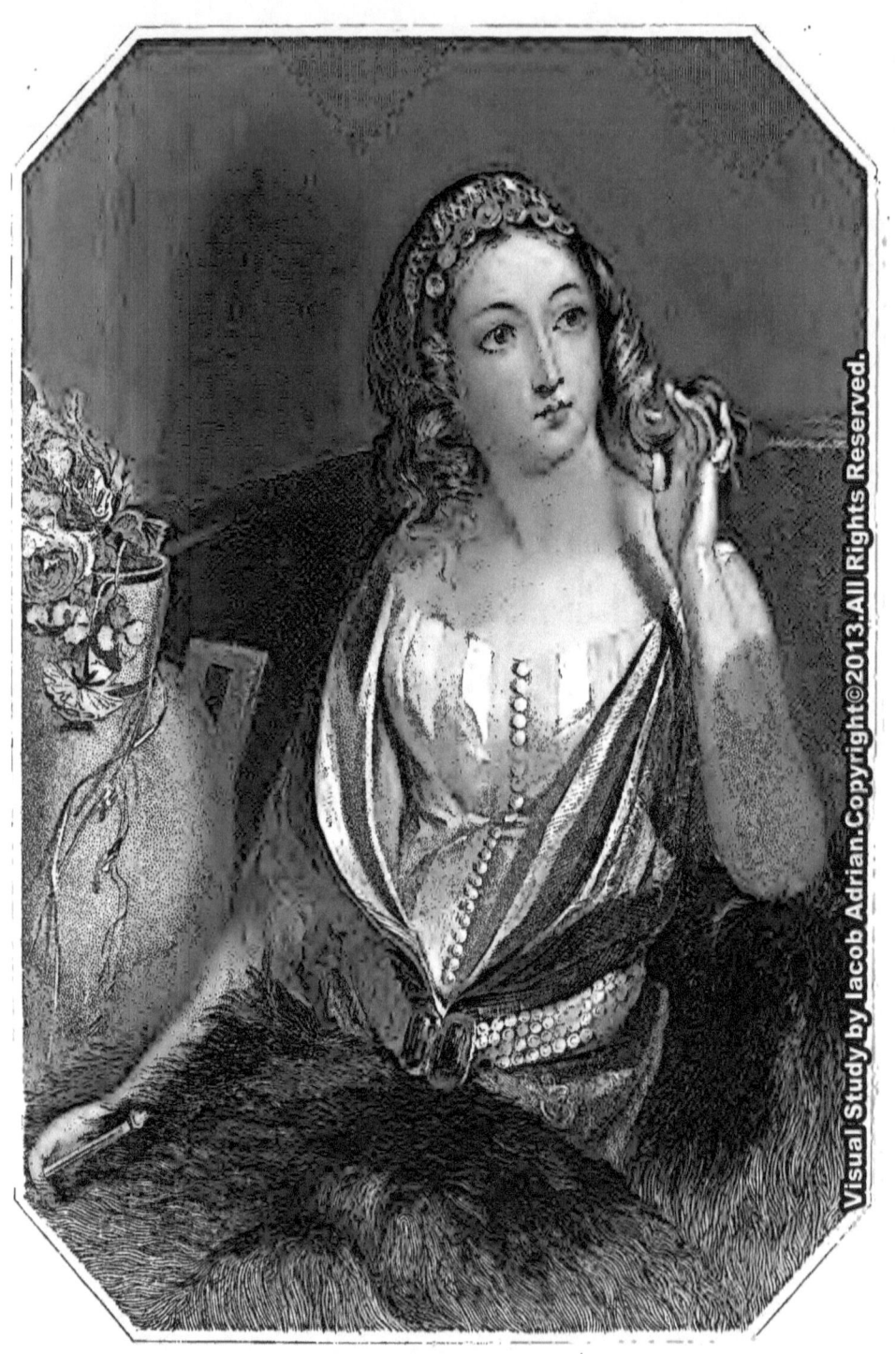

YOUNG HAIDEÉ.

THE YOUNG HAIDÉE.

THE Haidée here represented is not "the beauty of the Cyclades," but the subject of a Romaic love song, a great favourite with the young girls of Athens of all classes. Their manner of singing it is by verses in rotation, the whole number present joining in the chorus.

I.

I ENTER thy garden of roses,
    Beloved and fair Haidée,
Each morning where Flora reposes,
    For surely I see her in thee.
Oh, Lovely! thus low I implore thee,
    Receive this fond truth from my tongue,
Which utters its song to adore thee,
    Yet trembles for what it has sung;
As the branch, at the bidding of Nature,
    Adds fragrance and fruit to the tree,
Through her eyes, through her every feature,
    Shines the soul of the young Haidée.

II.

But the loveliest garden grows hateful
    When Love has abandon'd the bowers;
Bring me hemlock—since mine is ungrateful,
    That herb is more fragrant than flowers.

The poison, when pour'd from the chalice,
    Will deeply embitter the bowl;
But when drunk to escape from thy malice,
    The draught shall be sweet to my soul.
Too cruel! in vain I implore thee
    My heart from these horrors to save:
Will nought to my bosom restore thee?
    Then open the gates of the grave.

III.

As the chief who to combat advances
    Secure of his conquest before,
Thus thou, with those eyes for thy lances,
    Hast pierced through my heart to its core.
Ah, tell me, my soul! must I perish
    By pangs which a smile would dispel?
Would the hope, which thou once bad'st me cherish,
    For torture repay me too well?
Now sad is the garden of roses,
    Beloved but false Haidée!
There Flora all wither'd reposes,
    And mourns o'er thine absence with me.

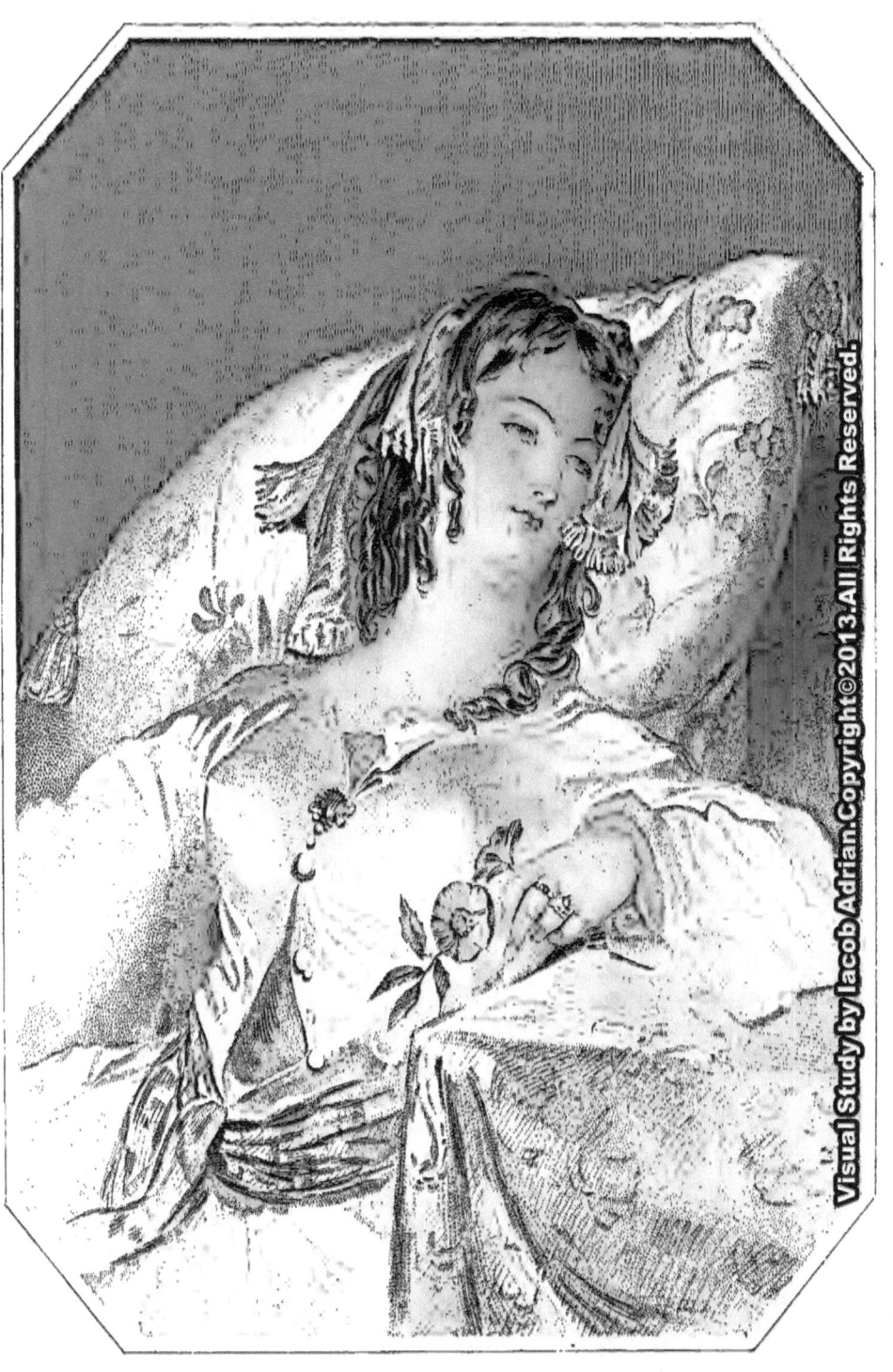

DUDÚ.

DUDU.

A KIND of sleepy Venus seem'd Dudu,
    Yet very fit to " murder sleep" in those
Who gazed upon her cheek's transcendant hue,
    Her Attic forehead, and her Phidian nose:
Few angles were there in her form, 'tis true,
    Thinner she might have been, and yet scarce lose;
Yet, after all, 'twould puzzle to say where
It would not spoil some separate charm to *pare*.

She was not violently lively, but
    Stole on your spirit like a May-day breaking;
Her eyes were not too sparkling, yet, half-shut,
    They put beholders in a tender taking;
She look'd (this simile's quite new) just cut
    From marble, like Pygmalion's statue waking,
The mortal and the marble still at strife,
And timidly expanding into life.

*   *   *   *   *   *

Dudù, as has been said, was a sweet creature,
　　Not very dashing, but extremely winning,
With the most regulated charms of feature,
　　Which painters cannot catch like faces sinning
Against proportion—the wild strokes of nature
　　Which they hit off at once in the beginning,
Full of expression, right or wrong, that strike,
And pleasing, or unpleasing, still are like.

But she was a soft landscape of mild earth,
　　Where all was harmony, and calm, and quiet,
Luxuriant, budding; cheerful without mirth,
　　Which, if not happiness, is much more nigh it
Than are your mighty passions and so forth,
　　Which, some call "the sublime;" I wish they'd try it:
.I've seen your stormy seas and stormy women,
And pity lovers rather more than seamen.

But she was pensive more than melancholy,
　　And serious more than pensive, and serene,
It may be, more than either—not unholy
　　Her thoughts, at least till now, appear to have been.
The strangest thing was, beauteous, she was wholly
　　Unconscious, albeit turn'd of quick seventeen,
That she was fair, or dark, or short, or tall;
She never thought about herself at all.

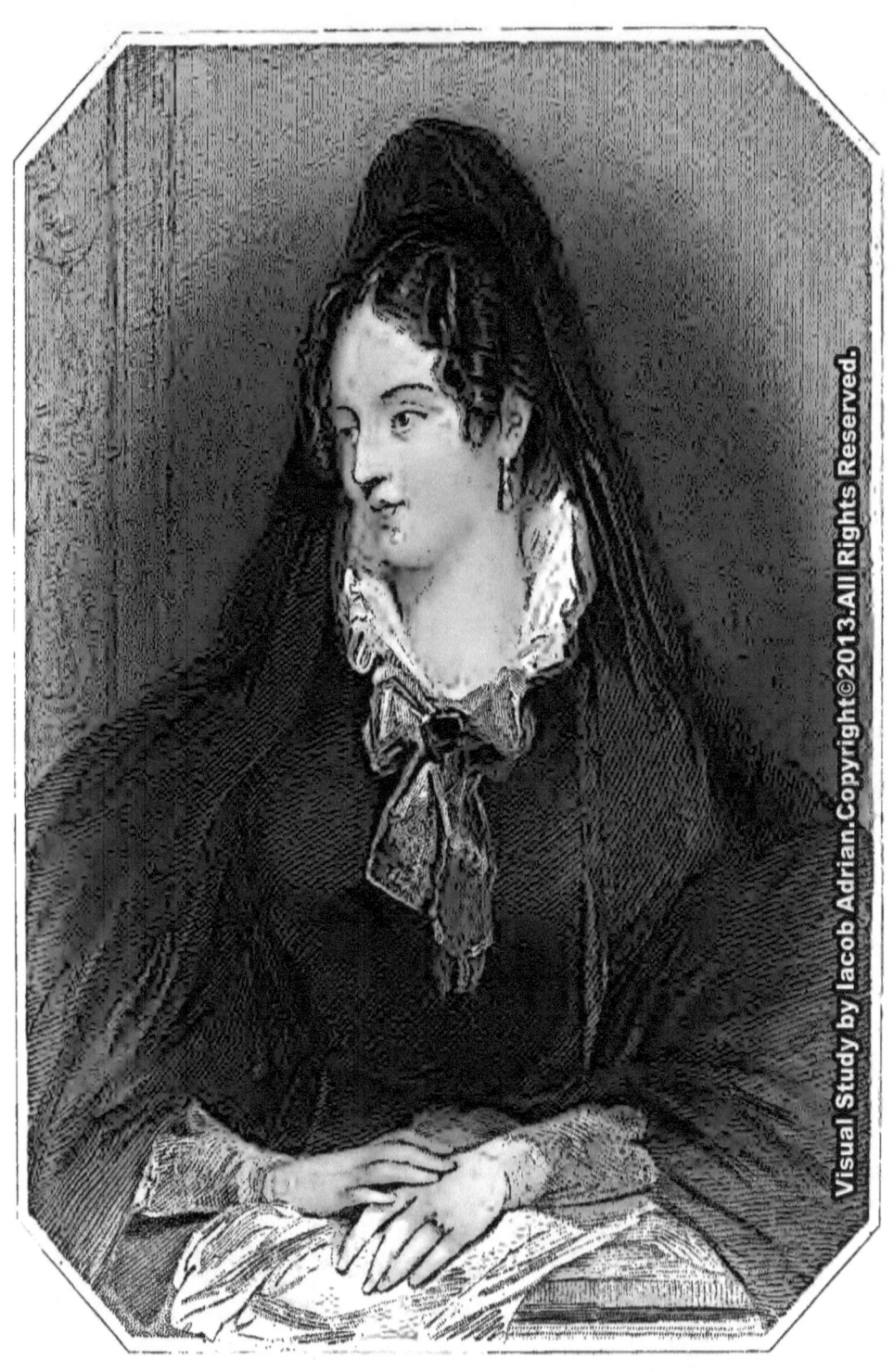

LADY · PINCHBECK.

LADY PINCHBECK.

JUAN, anxious to secure a guardian for the young orphan whom he had saved from slaughter at the taking of Ismail, makes choice of Lady Pinchbeck, from the many suitors anxious to take the management of the little Asiatic.

OLDEN she was—but had been very young;
   Virtuous she was—and had been, I believe;
Although the world has such an evil tongue
   That——but my chaster ear will not receive
An echo of a syllable that's wrong:
   In fact, there's nothing makes me so much grieve,
As that abominable tittle-tattle,
Which is the cud eschew'd by human cattle.

Moreover I've remark'd (and I was once
   A slight observer in a modest way),
And so may every one except a dunce,
   That ladies in their youth a little gay,
Besides their knowledge of the world, and sense
   Of the sad consequence of going astray,
Are wiser in their warnings 'gainst the woe
Which the mere passionless can never know.

*   *   *   *   *

LADY PINCHBECK.

I said that Lady Pinchbeck had been talk'd about—
   As who has not, if female, young and pretty?
But now no more the ghost of Scandal stalk'd about;
   She merely was deem'd amiable and witty,
And several of her best bon-mots were hawk'd about:
   Then she was given to charity and pity,
And pass'd (at least the latter years of life)
For being a most exemplary wife.

High in high circles, gentle in her own,
   She was the mild reprover of the young
Whenever—which means every day—they'd shown
   An awkward inclination to go wrong.
The quantity of good she did's unknown,
   Or at the least would lengthen out my song:
In brief, the little orphan of the East
Had raised an interest in her, which increased.

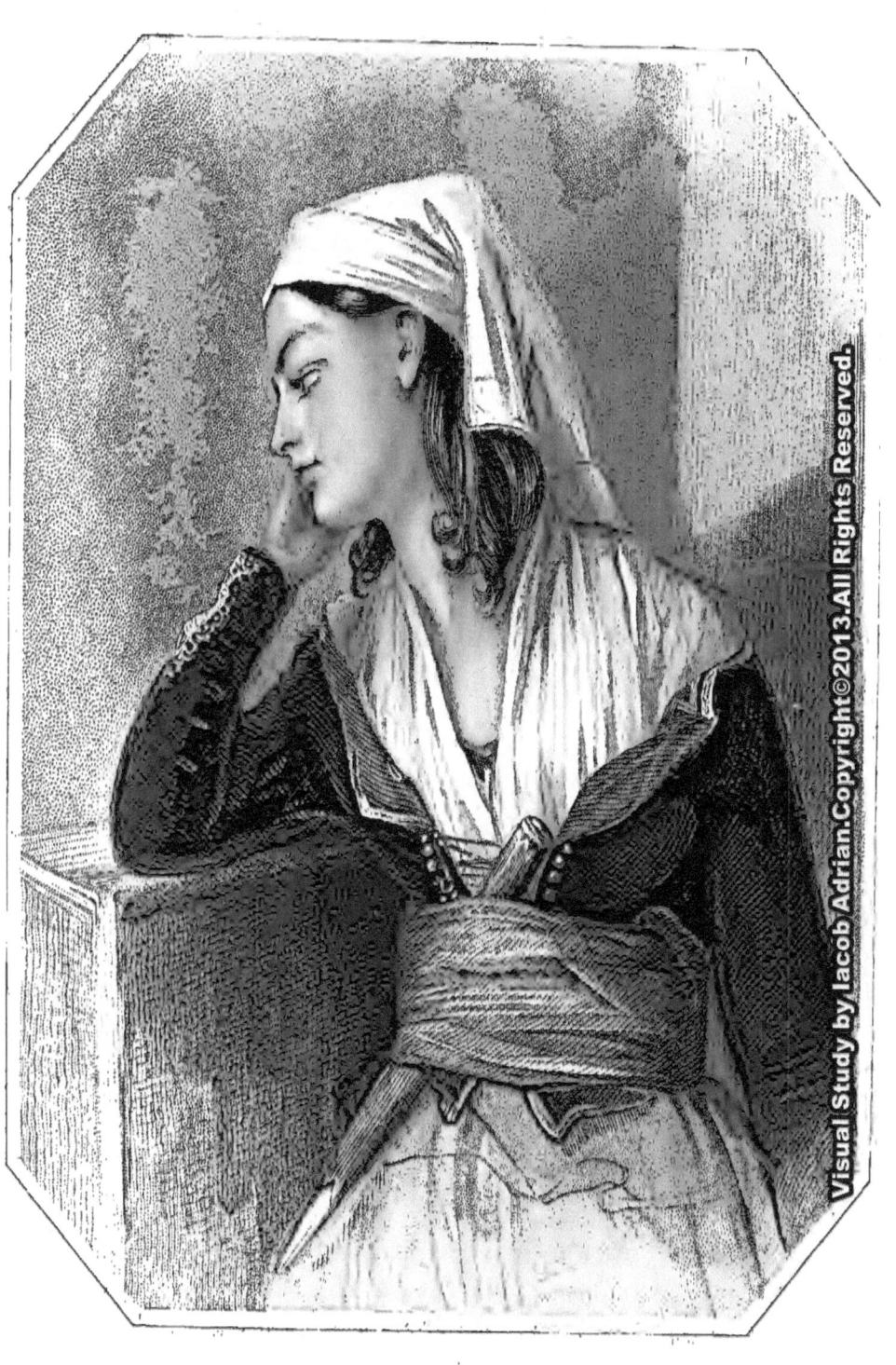

MAID OF SARAGOZA.

THE MAID OF SARAGOZA.

AND must they fall? the young, the proud, the brave,
To swell one bloated Chief's unwholesome reign?
No step between submission and a grave?
The rise of rapine and the fall of Spain?
And doth the Power that man adores ordain
Their doom, nor heed the suppliant's appeal?
Is all that desperate Valour acts in vain?
And Counsel sage, and patriotic Zeal,
The Veteran's skill, Youth's fire, and Manhood's heart of steel?

Is it for this the Spanish maid, aroused,
Hangs on the willow her unstrung guitar,
And, all unsex'd, the anlace hath espoused,
Sung the loud song, and dared the deed of war?
And she, whom once the semblance of a scar
Appall'd, an owlet's larum chill'd with dread,
Now views the column-scattering bay'net jar,
The falchion flash, and o'er the yet warm dead
Stalks with Minerva's step where Mars might quake to tread.

Ye who shall marvel when you hear her tale,
Oh! had you known her in her softer hour,
Mark'd her black eye that mocks her coal-black veil,
Heard her light, lively tones in Lady's bower,
Seen her long locks that foil the painter's power,

Her fairy form, with more than female grace,
Scarce would you deem that Saragoza's tower
Beheld her smile in Danger's Gorgon face,
Thin the closed ranks, and lead in Glory's fearful chase.

Her lover sinks—she sheds no ill-timed tear;
Her chief is slain—she fills his fatal post;
Her fellows flee—she checks their base career;
The foe retires—she heads the sallying host:
Who can appease like her a lover's ghost?
Who can avenge so well a leader's fall?
What maid retrieve when man's flush'd hope is lost?
Who hang so fiercely on the flying Gaul,
Foil'd by a woman's hand, before a batter'd wall?

" Such," says Lord Byron, " were the exploits of the Maid of Saragoza, who, by her valour, elevated herself to the highest rank of heroines. When the author was at Seville she walked daily on the Prado, decorated with medals and orders, by command of the Junta."

The exploits of Augustina, the famous heroine of both the sieges of Saragoza, are recorded at length in one of the most splendid chapters of Southey's History of the Peninsular War. At the time when she first attracted notice, by mounting a battery where her lover had fallen, and working a gun in his room, she was in her twenty-second year, exceedingly pretty, and in a soft feminine style of beauty. She has further had the honour to be painted by Wilkie, and alluded to in Wordsworth's Dissertation on the Convention of Cintra.

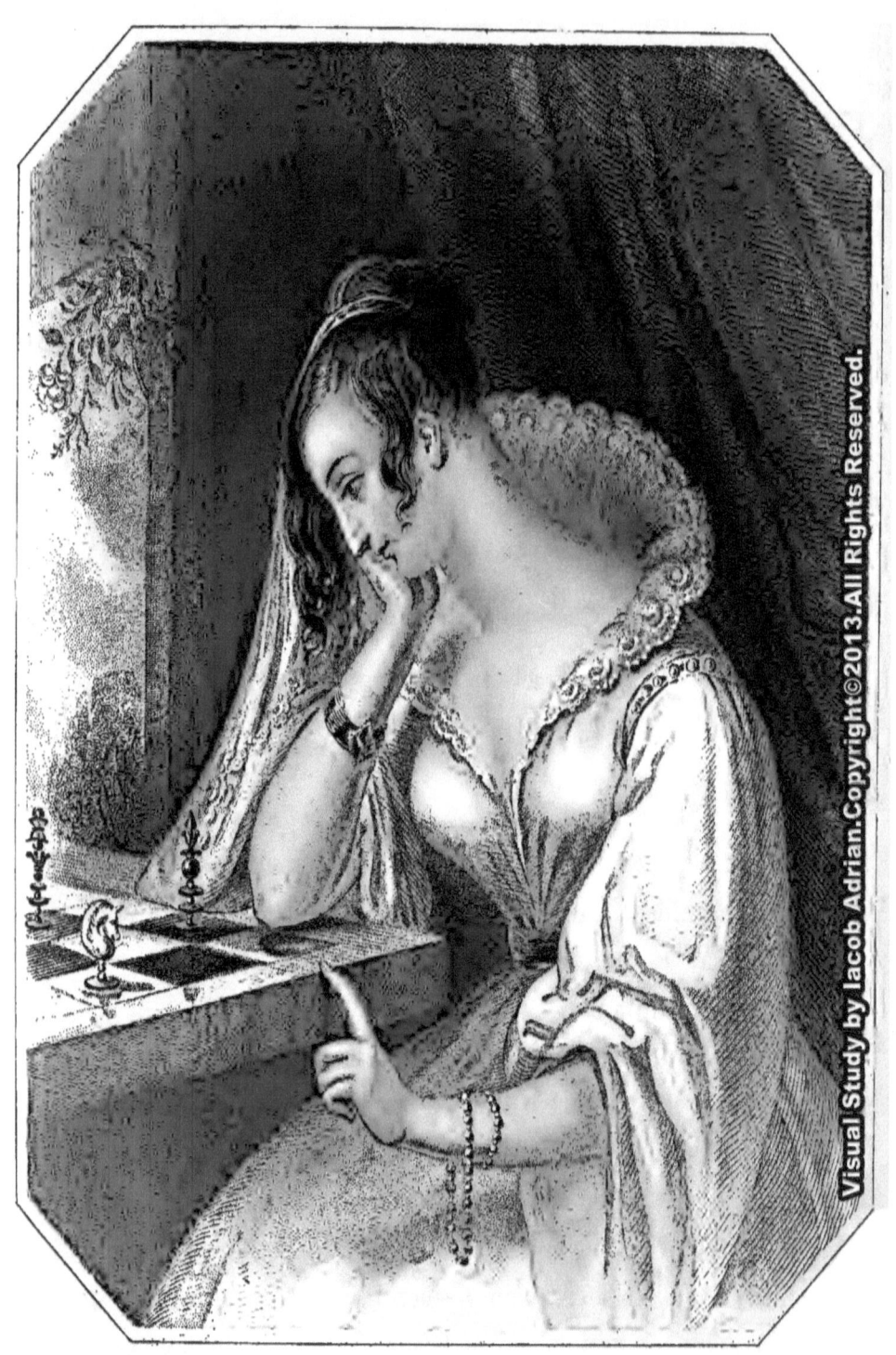

THERESA.

THERESA.

The story of Mazeppa is too well known to the admirers of Lord Byron's poetry to require a comment. Theresa, the object of the young page's attachment, is here represented as engaged with him in that—

> " Frivolous and foolish play,
> Wherewith they whiled away the day."

During its progress, Mazeppa suspected from the pre-occupation of his antagonist, that his passion was not utterly hopeless.

> " —— She was pensive, nor perceived
> Her occupation, nor was grieved,
> Nor glad to lose or gain ; but still
> Play'd on for hours, as if her will
> Yet bound her to the place, though not
> That hers might be the winning lot."

The sequel need not be told. The lines which follow have been selected as best describing the subject of the engraving.

> Theresa's form—
> Methinks it glides before me now,
> Between me and yon chestnut's bough,
> The memory is so quick and warm ;

And yet I find no words to tell
The shape of her I loved so well:
She had the Asiatic eye,
    Such as our Turkish neighbourhood
    Hath mingled with our Polish blood,
Dark as above us is the sky;
But through it stole a tender light,
Like the first moonrise of midnight;
Large, dark, and swimming in the stream,
Which seem'd to melt to its own beam;
All love, half-languor, and half fire,
Like saints that at the stake expire,
And lift their raptured looks on high,
As though it were a joy to die.
A brow like a midsummer lake,
    Transparent with the sun therein,
When waves no murmur dare to make,
    And heaven beholds her face within.
A cheek and lip—but why proceed?
    I loved her then—I love her still;
And such as I am, love indeed
    In fierce extremes—in good and ill.
But still we love even in our rage,
And haunted to our very age
With the vain shadow of the past,
As is Mazeppa to the last.

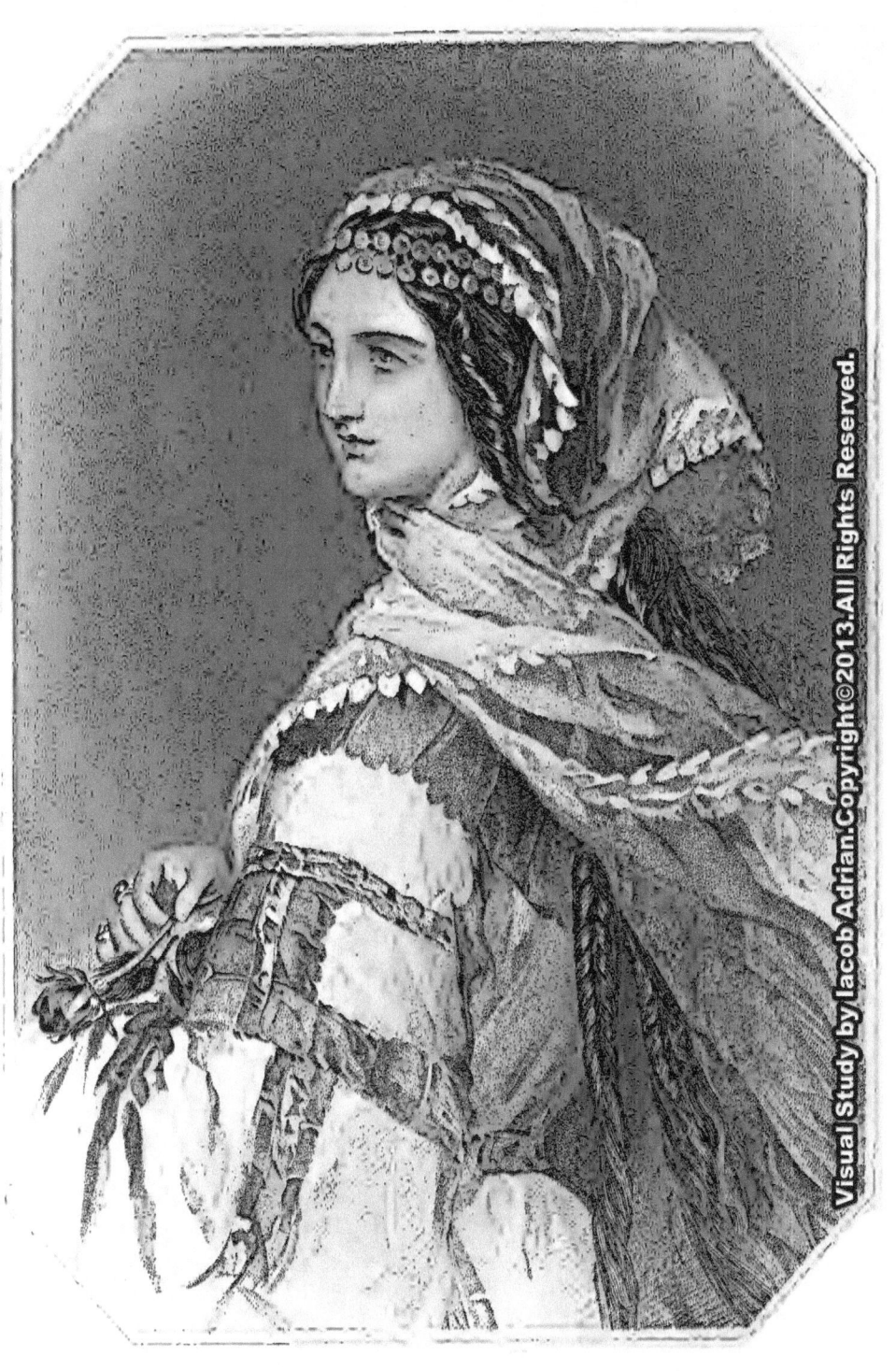

HAIDÉE.

HAIDÉE.

—◆—

SHIPWRECKED, and cast "like a withered lily" on the land,
Don Juan lay, "all doubt and dizziness," till waked from his
trance by a lovely and innocent girl, who, with her attendant,
found him on the beach, and lifting him into a cave, there tended
and restored him. This "gentle girl" was Haidée; and no
portion of this extraordinary poem is finished with so much
beauty as that which relates the loves of Juan and the fair Greek
girl. She is thus described :—

HER brow was overhung with coins of gold,
    That sparkled o'er the auburn of her hair,
Her clustering hair, whose longer locks were roll'd
    In braids behind; and though her stature were
Even of the highest for a female mould,
    They nearly reach'd her heel; and in her air
There was a something which bespoke command,
As one who was a lady in the land.

Her hair, I said, was auburn; but her eyes
    Were black as death, their lashes the same hue,
Of downcast length, in whose silk shadow lies
    Deepest attraction; for when to the view

Forth from its raven fringe the full glance flies,
   Ne'er with such force the swiftest arrow flew;
'Tis as the snake late coil'd, who pours his length,
And hurls at once his venom and his strength.

Her brow was white and low, her cheek's pure dye
   Like twilight rosy still with the set sun;
Short upper lip—sweet lips! that make us sigh
   Ever to have seen such; for she was one
Fit for the model of a statuary.

    *   *   *   *   *   *

   Her dress was very different from the Spanish,
Simpler, and yet of colours not so grave;
   For, as you know, the Spanish women banish
Bright hues when out of doors, and yet, while wave
   Around them (what I hope will never vanish)
The basquina and the mantilla, they
Seem at the same time mystical and gay.

But with our damsel this was not the case;
   Her dress was many-colour'd, finely spun;
Her locks curl'd negligently round her face,
   But through them gold and gems profusely shone:
Her girdle sparkled, and the richest lace
   Flow'd in her veil, and many a precious stone
Flash'd on her little hand; but, what was shocking,
Her small snow feet had slippers, but no stocking.

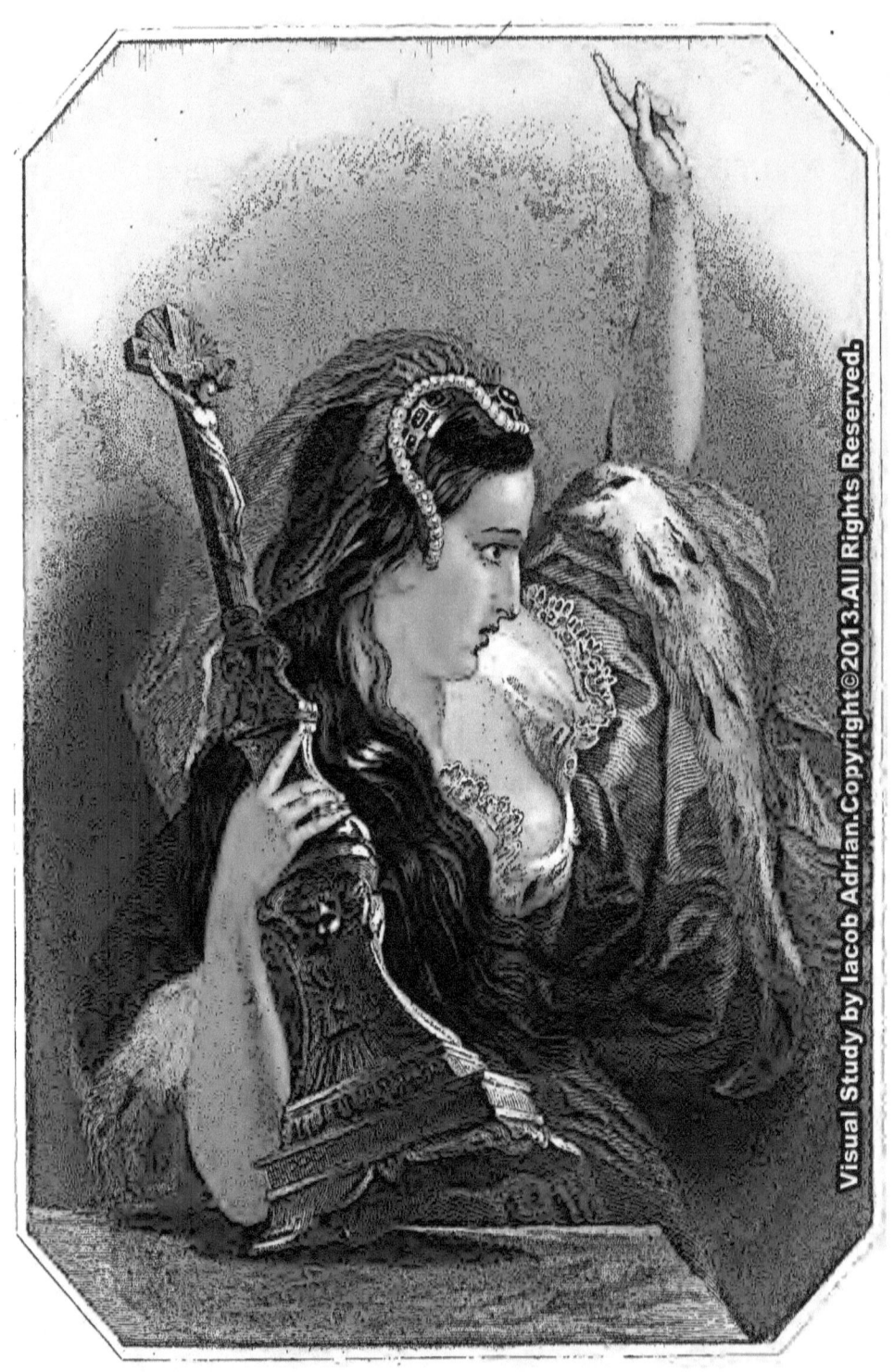

OLYMPIA.

OLIMPIA.

At the sacking of Rome by the troops of the Bourbon, Olimpia, a young and noble lady, flies for refuge to the high altar of St. Peter's, where, clinging to a golden cross, she threatens to hurl it on the heads of her pursuers. On the advance of one of the soldiers to seize her, she crushes him under the weight of the crucifix, and is about to forfeit her life to the revenge of his comrades, when she is rescued by Arnold, the " Deformed Transformed."

Enter Olimpia, *flying from the pursuit.—She springs upon the Altar.*

Soldier. She's mine!

Another Sold. (*opposing the former*). You lie, I track'd her first; and were she
The Pope's niece, I'll not yield her.   [*They fight.*

  3rd Sold. (*advancing towards* Olimpia). You may settle
Your claims; I'll make mine good.

  Olimpia.   Infernal slave!
You touch me not alive.

  3rd Sold.   Alive or dead!

Olimp. (*embracing a massive crucifix*).   Respect your God!

3rd Sold.   Yes, when he shines in gold.

Girl, you but grasp your dowry.

    [*As he advances,* OLIMPIA, *with a strong and sudden effort, casts down
       the crucifix : it strikes the Soldier, who falls.*

3rd Sold.   Oh, great God!

Olimp. Ah! now you recognise him.

3rd Sold.   My brain's crush'd !

Comrades, help, ho!   All's darkness !   [*He dies.*

   Other Soldiers (*coming up*). Slay her, although she had a thousand lives;
She hath kill'd our comrade.

   Olimp.   Welcome such a death !

You have no life to give, which the worst slave

Would take.   Great God! through thy redeeming Son.

And thy Son's Mother, now receive me as

I would approach thee, worthy her, and him, and thee !

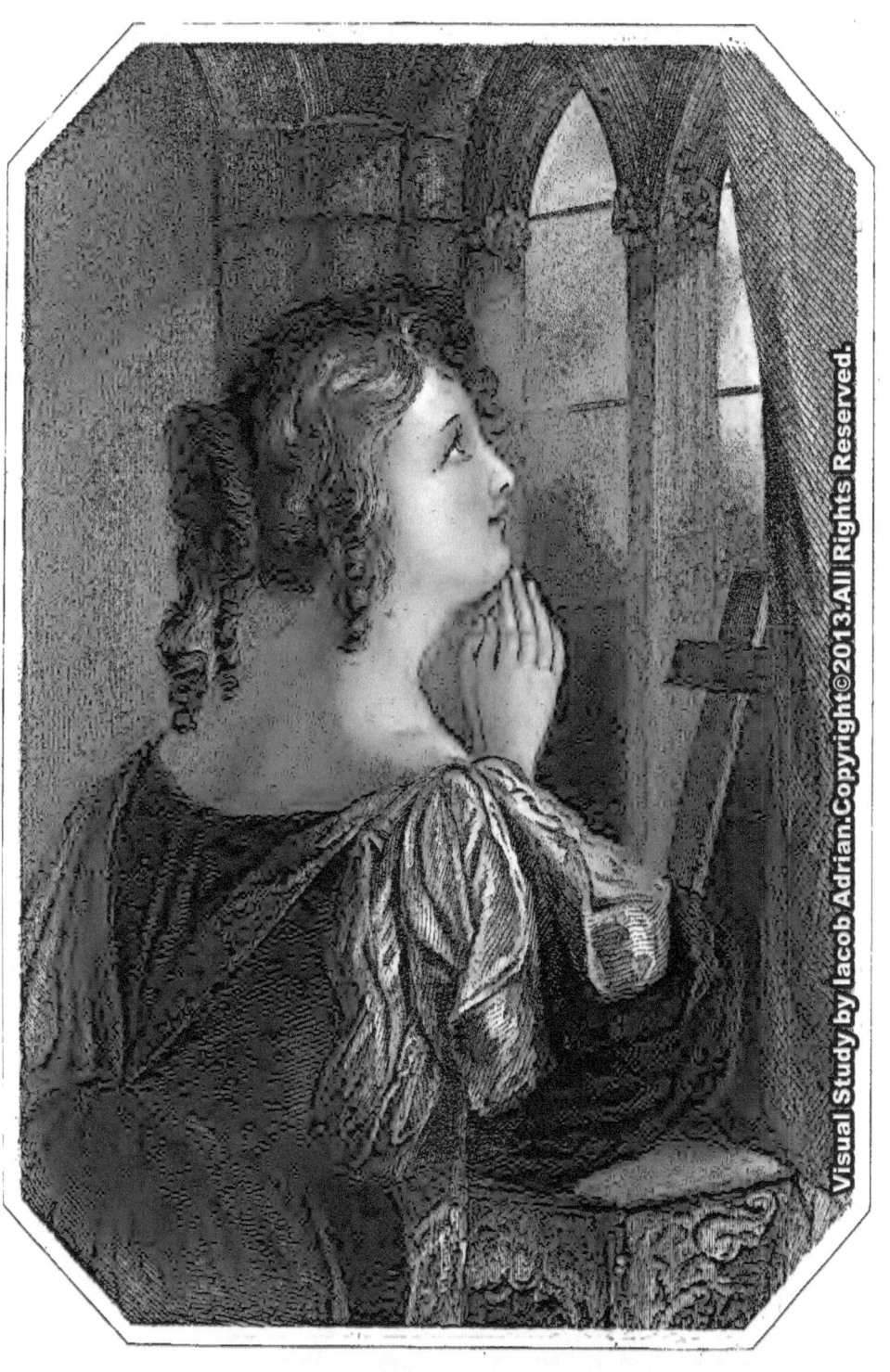

AURORA RABY.

AURORA RABY.

—◆—

ONE of the many guests assembled at Norman Abbey, was
Aurora Raby; but a being utterly distinct from those around
her; and, moving in an atmosphere of her own purity, heightening
by the contrast the worldliness of the lady Adeline, and the
voluptuousness of the "frolic duchess."

       There was
Indeed a certain fair and fairy one,
  Of the best class, and better than her class,
Aurora Raby, a young star who shone
  O'er life, too sweet an image for such glass,
A lovely being, scarcely form'd or moulded,
A rose with all its sweetest leaves yet folded;

Rich, noble, but an orphan : left an only
  Child to the care of guardians good and kind;
But still her aspect had an air so lonely!
  Blood is not water; and where shall we find
Feelings of youth like those which overthrown lie
  By death, when we are left, alas ! behind,
To feel, in friendless palaces, a home
Is wanting, and our best ties in the tomb ?

Early in years, and yet more infantine
   In figure, she had something of sublime
In eyes which sadly shone, as seraphs' shine.
    All youth—but with an aspect beyond time;
Radiant and grave—as pitying man's decline;
    Mournful—but mournful of another's crime,
She look'd as if she sat by Eden's door,
And grieved for those who could return no more.

She was a Catholic, too, sincere, austere,
   As far as her own gentle heart allow'd,
And deem'd that fallen worship far more dear
    Perhaps because 'twas fallen: her sires were proud
Of deeds and days when they had fill'd the ear
    Of nations, and had never bent or bow'd
To novel power; and as she was the last,
She held their old faith and old feelings fast.

She gazed upon a world she scarcely knew
   As seeking not to know it; silent, lone,
As grows a flower, thus quietly she grew,
    And kept her heart serene within its zone.
There was awe in the homage which she drew;
    Her spirit seem'd as seated on a throne
Apart from the surrounding world, and strong
In its own strength—most strange in one so young!

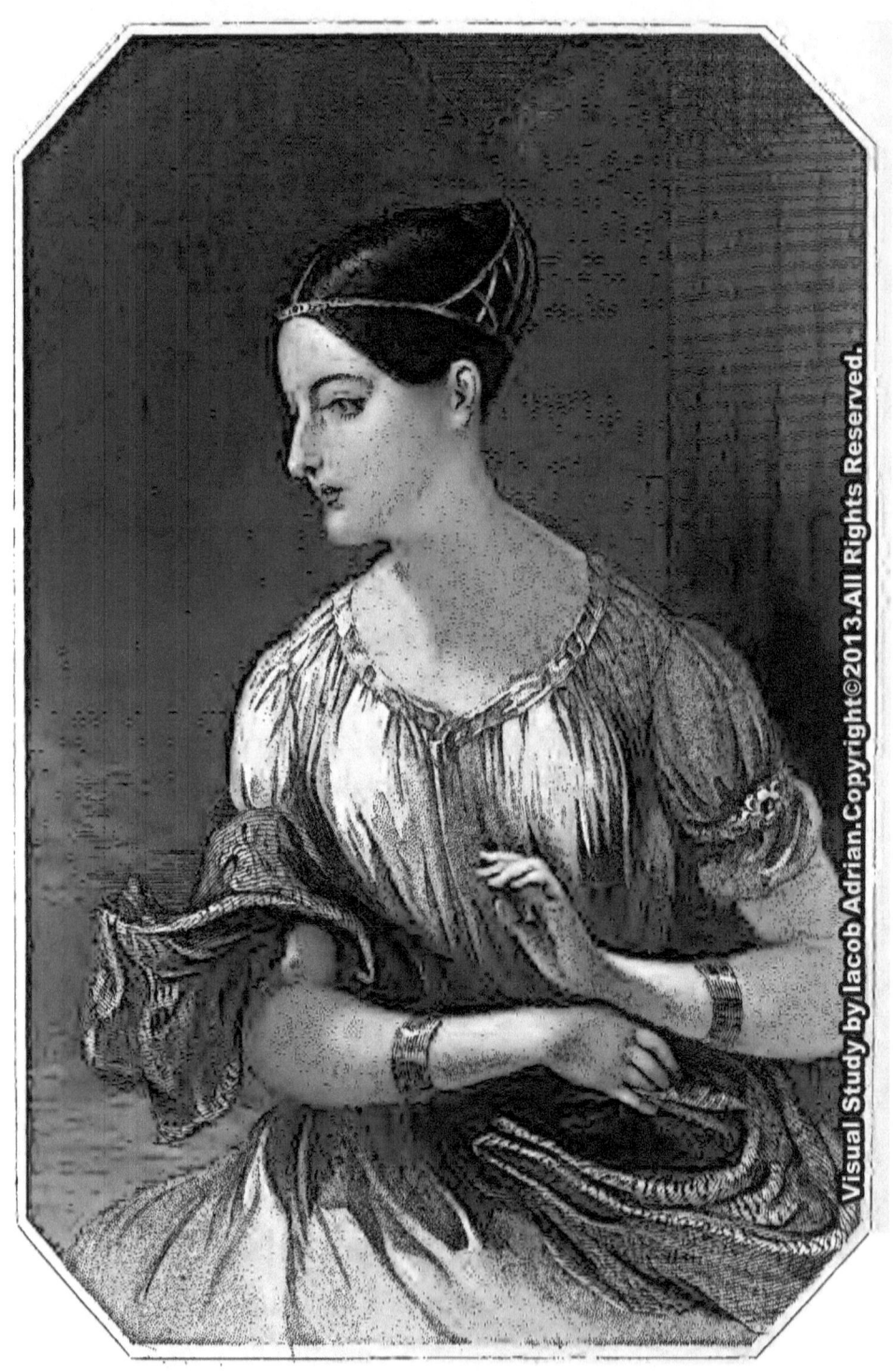

MYRRHA.

MYRRHA.

———✦———

" THE chief charm and vivifying angel of the piece," says
Jeffrey, "is Myrrha, the Greek slave of Sardanapalus, a beautiful,
heroic, devoted, and ethereal being, in love with the generous and
infatuated monarch, ashamed of loving a barbarian, and using all
her influence over him to ennoble as well as adorn his existence,
and to arm him against the terrors of his close. Her voluptuousness is that of the heart, her heroism of the affections." The
"eloquent Ionian" is represented in the engraving as watching
over the slumbers of Sardanapalus, disturbed and agitated by
horrid dreams.

> *Myrrha.* I HAVE stolen upon his rest, if rest it be,
> Which thus convulses slumber: shall I wake him?
> No, he seems calmer. Oh, thou God of Quiet!
> Whose reign is o'er seal'd eyelids and soft dreams,
> Or deep, deep sleep, so as to be unfathom'd,
> Look like thy brother, Death,—so still—so stirless—
> For then we are happiest, as it may be, we
> Are happiest of all within the realm
> Of thy stern, silent, and unwakening twin.

MYRRHA.

Again he moves—again the play of pain
Shoots o'er his features, as the sudden gust
Crisps the reluctant lake that lay so calm
Beneath the mountain shadow; or the blast
Ruffles the autumn leaves, that drooping cling
Faintly and motionless to their loved boughs.
I must awake him—yet not yet: who knows
From what I rouse him? It seems pain; but if
I quicken him to heavier pain? The fever
Of this tumultuous night, the grief too of
His wound, though slight, may cause all this, and shake
Me more to see than him to suffer. No:
Let Nature use her own maternal means,—
And I await to second, not disturb her.

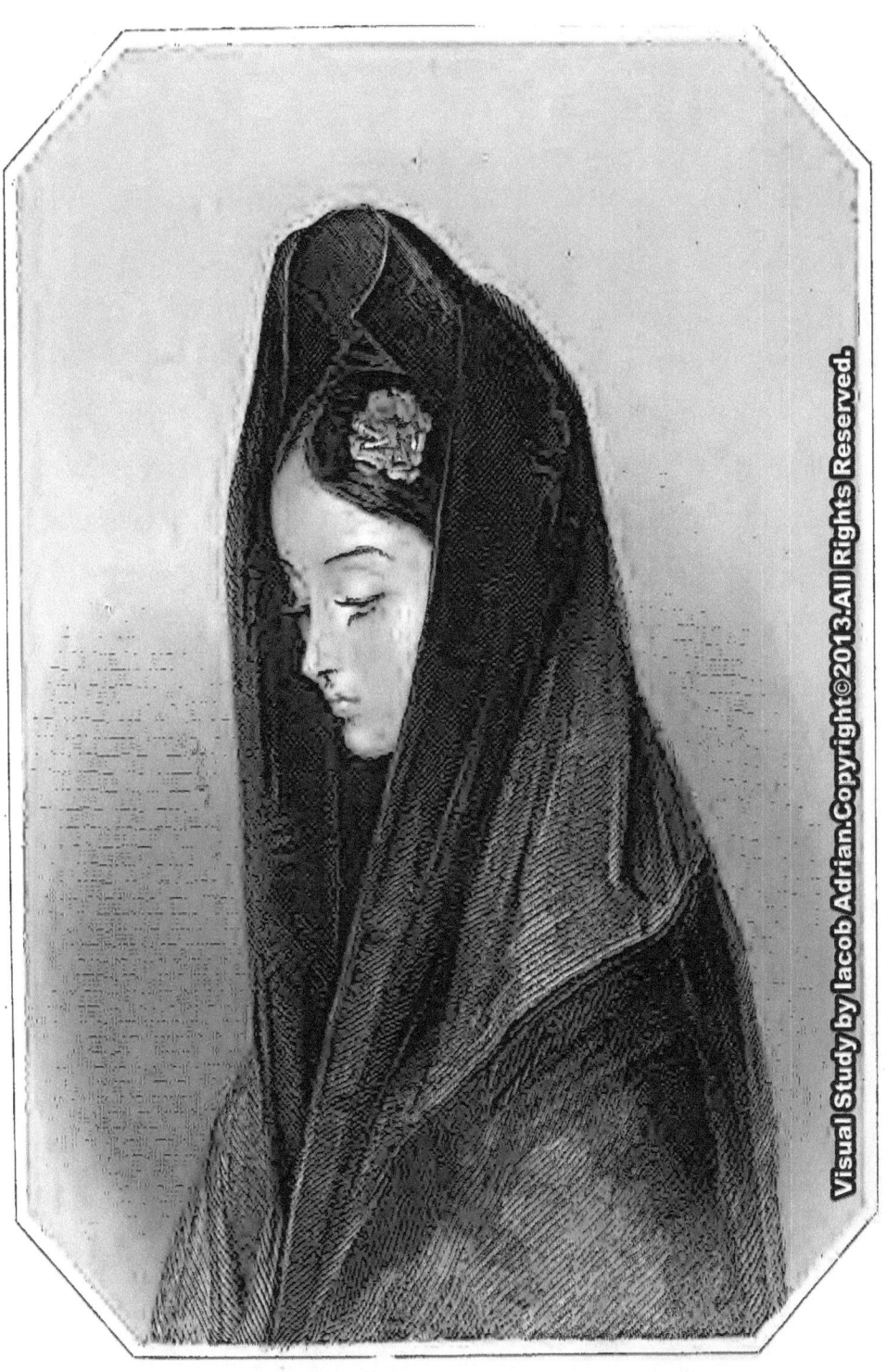

DONNA INEZ.

DONNA INEZ.

—◆—

DONNA INEZ, the mother of the far-famed Don Juan, is one of the most elaborately finished characters in the poem of that name. Nothing can be more repulsive than her mental perfections, accompanied, as they are, by the hypocrisy which conceals —not immorality, but heartlessness—not vice, but the absence of virtue. Her quarrels with Don José, on suspicion of his infidelity, though herself "in the same condemnation," we pardon, as being a natural ebullition of feminine spleen ; but we cannot so easily forgive her for her appropriation of the husband of her friend,— that friend being "selected for discretion and devotion,"—nor for the *pious* letter, in which she commends her son to heaven and to the *maternal* love of the Empress.

> His mother was a learned lady, famed
>   For every branch of every science known—
> In every Christian language ever named,
>   With virtues equall'd by her wit alone ;
> She made the cleverest people quite ashamed,
>   And even the good with inward envy groan,
> Finding themselves so very much exceeded
> In their own way by all the things that she did.

DONNA INEZ.

Her memory was a mine: she knew by heart
    All Calderon and greater part of Lopé,
So that if any actor miss'd his part
    She could have served him for the prompter's copy;
For her Feinagle's were an useless art,
    And he himself obliged to shut up shop—he
Could never make a memory so fine as
That which adorn'd the brain of Donna Inez.

Her favourite science was the mathematical,
    Her noblest virtue was her magnanimity,
Her wit (she sometimes tried at wit) was Attic all,
    Her serious sayings darken'd to sublimity;
In short, in all things she was fairly what I call
    A prodigy—her morning dress was dimity,
Her evening silk, or, in the summer, muslin,
And other stuffs, with which I won't stay puzzling.

*   *   *   *   *   *

Oh! she was perfect past all parallel—
    Of any modern female saint's comparison;
So far above the cunning power of hell,
    Her guardian angel had given up his garrison;
Even her minutest motions went as well
    As those of the best time-piece made by Harrison:
In virtues nothing earthly could surpass her,
Save thine " incomparable oil," Macassar!

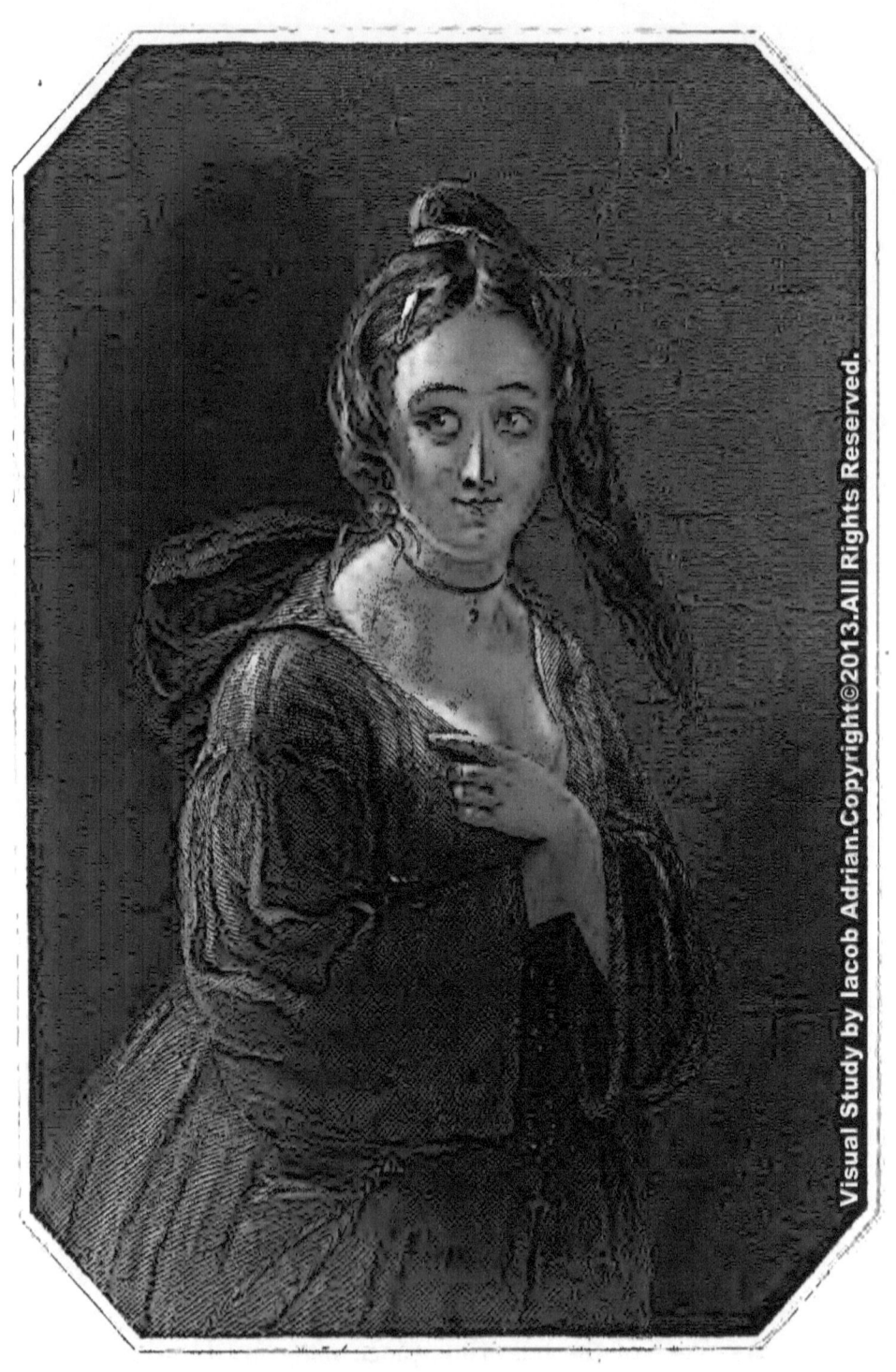

THE DUCHESS OF FITZFULKE.

THE DUCHESS OF FITZ-FULKE.

THE legend of the Grey Friar, sung by the Lady Adeline, and the supposition arising from the paleness of Juan's countenance, and the disorder of his manner, that he had been visited by the apparition of the Monk, induce " her gracious, graceful, graceless grace," the full-grown Hebe of Fitz-Fulke, to personate the phantom of the Friar.   The jest is discovered by the resolution with which the young Spaniard follows up the adventure.

DON JUAN, when the midnight hour of pillows
   Arrived, retired to his ; but to despond
Rather than rest.   Instead of poppies, willows
   Waved o'er his couch ; he meditated, fond
Of those sweet bitter thoughts which banish sleep,
And make the worldling sneer, the youngling weep.

     *   *   *   *   *   *   *

The door flew wide, not swiftly,—but, as fly
   The sea-gulls, with a steady, sober flight—
And then swung back ; nor close—but stood awry,
   Half letting in long shadows on the light,
Which still in Juan's candlesticks burn'd high,
   For he had two, both tolerably bright,
And in the door-way, darkening darkness, stood
The sable friar in his solemn hood

     *   *   *   *   *   *   *

Juan put forth one arm—Eternal powers !
　It touch'd no soul, nor body, but the wall,
On which the moonbeams fell in silvery showers,
　Chequer'd with all the tracery of the hall ;
He shudder'd, as no doubt the bravest cowers
　When he can't tell what 'tis that doth appal.
How odd, a single hobgoblin's non-entity
Should cause more fear than a whole host's identity.

But still the shade remain'd : the blue eyes glared,
　And rather variably for stony death :
Yet one thing rather good the grave had spared,
　The ghost had a remarkably sweet breath.
A straggling curl show'd he had been fair-hair'd ;
　A red lip with two rows of pearls beneath,
Gleam'd forth, as through the casement's ivy shroud
The moon peep'd, just escaped from a grey cloud.

And Juan, puzzled, but still curious, thrust
　His other arm forth—Wonder upon wonder !
It press'd upon a hard but glowing bust,
　Which beat as if there was a warm heart under.
He found, as people on most trials must,
　That he had made at first a silly blunder,
And that in his confusion he had caught
Only the wall, instead of what he sought.

The ghost, if ghost it were, seem'd a sweet soul
　As ever lurk'd beneath a holy hood :
A dimpled chin, a neck of ivory, stole
　Forth into something much like flesh and blood
Back fell the sable frock and dreary cowl,
　And they reveal'd—alas ! that e'er they should !
In full, voluptuous, but *not o'er*-grown bulk,
The phantom of her frolic Grace—Fitz-Fulke !

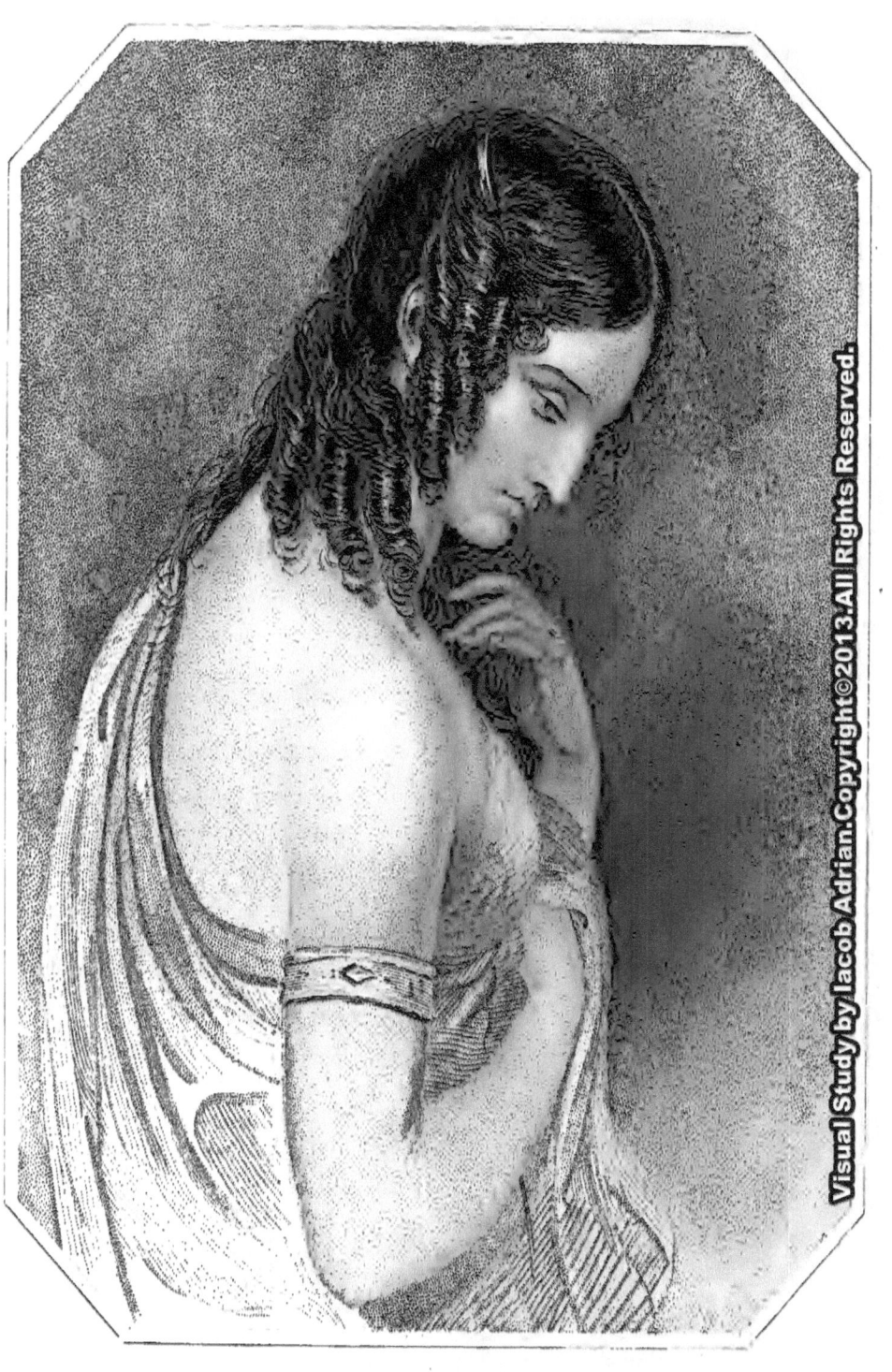

ASTARTE.

ASTARTE.

"OVER the fine drama of Manfred," says Professor Wilson, "a moral feeling hangs like a sombrous thunder-cloud. No other guilt but that so darkly shadowed out could have furnished so dreadful an illustration of the hideous aberrations of human nature, however noble and majestic, when left a prey to its desires, its passions, and its imagination. We think of Astarte as young, beautiful, innocent—guilty—lost—murdered—buried —judged—pardoned; but still, in her permitted visit to earth, speaking in a voice of sorrow, and with a countenance yet pale with mortal trouble. The moral breathes and burns in every word,—in sadness, misery, insanity, desolation, and death."

Manfred. CAN this be death? there's bloom upon her cheek;
But now I see it is no living hue
But a strange hectic—like the unnatural red
Which Autumn plants upon the perish'd leaf.
It is the same! Oh, God! that I should dread
To look upon the same—Astarte!   *   *

*   *   *   *   *   *   *

                         Hear me, hear me—
Astarte! my beloved! speak to me:
I have so much endured—so much endure—
Look on me! the grave hath not changed thee more
Than I am changed for thee. Thou lovedst me
Too much, as I loved thee: we were not made
To torture thus each other, though it were
The deadliest sin to love as we have loved.
Say that thou loath'st me not—that I do bear
This punishment for both—that thou wilt be

One of the blessed—and that I shall die ;
For hitherto all hateful things conspire
To bind me in existence—in a life
Which makes me shrink from immortality—
A future like the past.   I cannot rest.
I know not what I ask, nor what I seek .
I feel but what thou art—and what I am:
And I would hear yet once before I perish
The voice which was my music—Speak to me !
For I have call'd on thee in the still night,
Startled the slumbering birds from the hush'd boughs,
And woke the mountain wolves, and made the caves
Acquainted with thy vainly echoed name,
Which answer'd me—many things answer'd me—
Spirits and men—but thou wert silent all.
Yet speak to me ! I have outwatch'd the stars,
And gazed o'er heaven in vain in search of thee.
Speak to me ! I have wander'd o'er the earth,
And never found thy likeness—Speak to me !
Look on the fiends around—they feel for me :
I fear them not, and feel for thee alone—
Speak to me ! though it be in wrath ;—but say—
I reck not what—but let me hear thee once—
This once—once more !

    Phantom of Astarte. Manfred !
    Man.   Say on, say on—
I live but in the sound—it is thy voice !
    Phan. Manfred ! To-morrow ends thine earthly ills.
Farewell !
    Man. Yet one word more—am I forgiven ?
    Phan. Farewell !
    Man.   Say, shall we meet again ?
    Phan. Farewell !
    Man. One word for mercy ! Say, thou lovest me.
    Phan. Manfred !

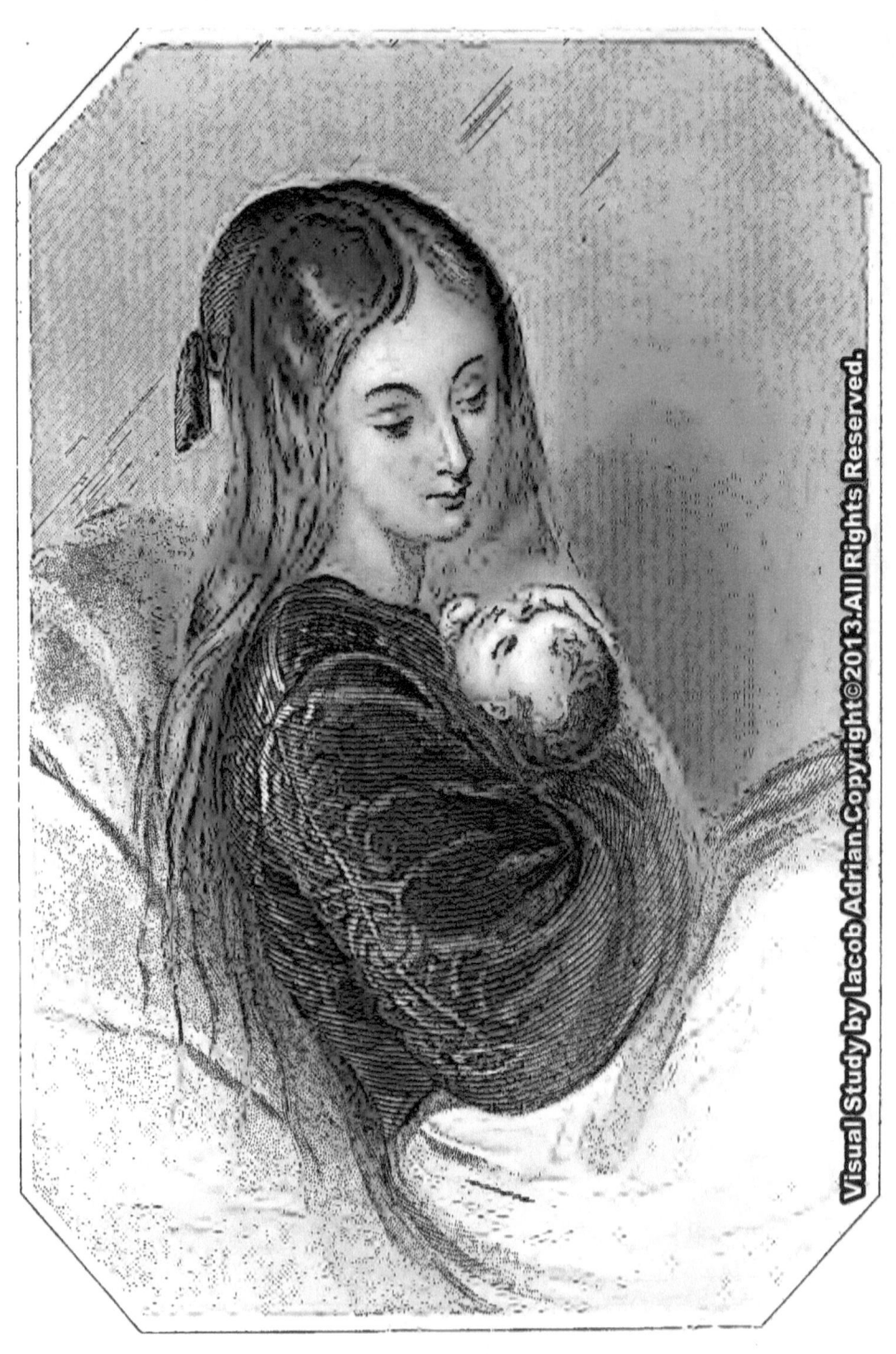

LIGHT OF THE HAREM.

THE LIGHT OF THE HAREM.

"LORD BYRON," says Mr. Jeffrey, "has made a fine use of the gentleness and submission of the Eastern females, as contrasted with the lordly pride and martial ferocity of the men; and though, we suspect, he has lent them more *soul* than of right belongs to them, as well as more delicacy and reflection, yet, there is something so true to female nature in general, in his representations of this sort, and so much of the Oriental softness and acquiescence in his particular delineations, that it is scarcely possible to refuse the picture the praise of being characteristic and harmonious, as well as eminently sweet and beautiful in itself."

> Apart,
> And scarce permitted, guarded, veil'd, to move,
> She yields to one her person and her heart,
> Tamed to her cage, nor feels a wish to rove:
> For, not unhappy in her master's love,
> And joyful in a mother's gentlest cares,
> Blest cares! all other feelings far above!
> Herself more sweetly rears the babe she bears,
> Who never quits the breast, no meaner passion shares.

The Harem, of which the annexed portrait was "the Light," formed part of the establishment of Ali Pacha, that "man of war and woes."

Bibliographic sources :

The gallery of Byron beauties;
portraits of the principal female characters
in Lord Byron's poems.
From original paintings by eminent artists ([n.d.])

Author:
Byron, George Gordon Byron, Baron, 1788-1824

Publisher: London D. Bogue